Two Revolutions
and the Constitution

Two Revolutions and the Constitution

How the English and American Revolutions Produced the American Constitution

James D. R. Philips

HAMILTON BOOKS
Lanham • Boulder • New York • London

Published by Hamilton Books
An imprint of The Rowman & Littlefield Publishing Group, Inc.
4501 Forbes Boulevard, Suite 200, Lanham, Maryland 20706
www.rowman.com

6 Tinworth Street, London SE11 5AL, United Kingdom

British Library Cataloguing in Publication Information Available

Library of Congress Cataloging-in-Publication Data

Library of Congress Control Number: 2021932009

ISBN: 9780761872689 (pbk: alk. paper)
ISBN: 9780761872696 (electronic)

♾™ The paper used in this publication meets the minimum requirements of
American National Standard for Information Sciences—Permanence of Paper
for Printed Library Materials, ANSI/NISO Z39.48-1992.

To Julie

Contents

Acknowledgments

For those parts of this book dealing directly with constitutional developments, especially American constitutional developments, I was able to work from copies of the original documents. I am indebted to all the platforms that have made available, online, the primary documents referred to in the Bibliography and Further Reading sections. I must especially acknowledge the outstanding collection of The Avalon Project of the Yale Law School, Lillian Goldman Law Library (in memory of Sol Goldman). I am grateful to the Goldmans and to everyone who has worked on The Avalon Project.

The drafting and implementation of the American Constitution is one of the most important events in the development of the contemporary world because it enabled and propagated republican, constitutional, pluralistic, representative government. The invention of the Constitution has, of course, been written about on many occasions from different perspectives and with a focus on different issues. I am indebted to all the scholars and writers whose work on American topics is referred to in the Bibliography and Further Reading sections of this book.

The English and British have been less interested in their constitution, perhaps, in part, because it is not codified and may therefore seem amorphous. Brexit and the excising of the powers of the European Union from the British constitution provides an opportunity to codify it. That would make its terms more accessible and less uncertain. But it is difficult to see any political dividend for a government that undertook such a project.

My interest in the English revolutionary period was sparked by Geoffrey Robertson's remarkable *The Tyrannicide Brief*. That book makes a compelling case for the trial and execution of Charles I as a defining event in the development of modern constitutional government (and as a foundation of the modern law of crimes against humanity). I am indebted to all the writers and scholars on English and British topics whose work is referred to in the Bibliography and Further Reading sections of this book.

One person helped me up-close throughout this project: my wife, Julie Claridge. I am grateful to her for her invaluable advice on the manuscript and for her unstinting, generous encouragement and counsel throughout the process of my researching and writing this book.

Several people reviewed a draft of the manuscript or provided me with other helpful comments or assistance. Thank you, Margaret Taylor, Tom Switzer, Simon Bates, Ed Day, Ashish Diwan, Tom Philips, Costas Condoleon, Andrew Pickford, Charmaine Chow, Greg Lindsay, Lachlan Philips, David Libling, and John M. Green. Mark Malatesta provided valuable guidance on the process of seeking a publisher.

I alone am responsible for any errors.

Introduction

The American Constitution is America's fundamental law. Its adoption established a revolutionary new system of government, secured the gains of the American Revolution, and enabled the American nation. It is of daily relevance to Americans because it established America's current system of government and law.

Why does the Constitution provide for a partly national and partly federal system? Why does it establish three branches of government (Congress, the President, and the Courts) and allocate separate powers to each of them? Why does it check and balance the different branches, including giving Congress the power to impeach? Why does it provide for elections, and for the electoral college?

The answers are found in the history that produced the American Revolution, and in the brilliant adaptations and innovations in the system of government developed by the Framers.

Before the American Revolutionary period, Americans thought that the British constitution was the best in the world. Under the British system and their colonial charters, Americans already enjoyed greater liberties and opportunities than any other people, including those in Britain.

Once they declared independence in 1776, the former British colonies in America needed their own rules for a new system of government. They drafted and adopted State constitutions. They needed co-operation between the States to fight the British, so the new States tried a confederation. It was too weak, so eleven years after declaring independence, the Framers devised a revolutionary federal and national constitution—the first major written constitution of the modern world.

The new State and federal constitutions and the system of law were deeply influenced by the British system, but with brilliant and revolutionary changes.

Americans removed the British monarch and entrenched their freedoms in an innovative scheme that was tyrant-proof and uniquely American. It was built on the sovereignty of the American people rather than the sovereignty of a king or queen.

So, as well as describing the American Revolution and the development of the American constitutions that came before the final Constitution, this book tells the story of the revolutionary development of the English system of law and government that was a foundation of the American system.

"Habeas corpus" (the right to prevent unlawful or arbitrary imprisonment) began as a power of the king to prevent his subjects being unlawfully detained by local noblemen.

"No taxation without representation," the most famous slogan attributed to the Revolutionary period, is a principle that dates back at least to the ancient Magna Carta.

When the English tried and executed their King Charles I, they were insisting that the King was subject to Parliament and to the law. The President is subject to constitutional checks and to law.

When Parliament installed a new King and Queen (William and Mary) to replace the rash James II, it also passed a Bill of Rights entrenching many ancient English liberties. The American Bill of Rights was added to the Constitution almost immediately after it was ratified.

Meanwhile the common law—laws that had been developed by the people and judges and not handed down by a monarch or legislature—was imported from England and gradually adapted in America, as a bulwark of protections of individuals and their property.

In the earliest of their new constitutions (which were State constitutions) the Founders opted for frequent elections, strong legislatures, and weak executives. They knew from British history that before the English (or "Glorious") Revolution, kings had sometimes delayed elections, convened Parliaments infrequently, and governed with little control by Parliament.

Experience in the late 1770s and early 1780s taught Americans that they had overreacted in their first State constitutions. And their first attempt at a confederation of all the States was dangerously impotent.

By the time of drafting the final American Constitution in 1787, the Framers chose a new balance. Elections were less frequent than under the first State constitutions, the legislature (Congress) checked but did not overwhelm the executive, and the executive branch was vested in the powerful new office of President. But the President was subject to an allocation of powers, checks by Congress, and the rule of law. Congress had a role in enforcing the rule of law against the President (by impeachment), and so did a new and powerful federal judiciary.

The story told in this book includes why and how the first State constitutions were drafted, the devastating frustrations of the Confederation and its constitution (the "Articles of Confederation"), and how the Constitutional Convention at Philadelphia produced the remarkable final Constitution.

It does not diminish the greatness of the achievement of the American Framers to understand the British system of government and law under which colonial America had thrived and which influenced the new constitutions, but with revolutionary changes. The English influence on the Constitution was acknowledged in impeachment proceedings against President Trump when, on December 4, 2019, the House Judiciary Committee heard from four law professors. Three of them referred to the British origins of impeachment.

Of course, the American Constitution had its flaws and anomalies. Most obviously, it did not outlaw slavery, notwithstanding the assertion in the Declaration of Independence[1] that ". . . all Men are created equal, that they are endowed by their Creator with certain unalienable Rights . . ." Many contemporaries, including slave owners at the convention that drafted the Constitution, recognized this aberration. Because of the economic dependence of the South on slavery, it would have been impossible to form a union of the thirteen founding States and to prohibit slavery. But the Constitution, the Bill of Rights and the common law established such a robust framework for personal rights that eventually progress was made in eliminating slavery and other areas of legal inequality.

One of the most remarkable aspects of the history that produced the Constitution is how fortunate, for the Americans, the British King's timing was in his violation of American liberties. By the 1760s Americans had enjoyed their special freedoms for several generations. They had prospered, and their population was large enough for resistance to the British to seem possible. They had combined their individualistic religious values with new theories of politics, which allowed revolution if a ruler was oppressing the people. Rebellion and revolution would have been less credible and likely if George III and the British Parliament had tightened the screws on Americans much earlier than they did. We should not read history backwards and treat what occurred as inevitable. At many points, the story told in this book could have taken a different direction.

Constitutions are legal documents that establish systems of government and law. But this book is not dense in legal detail. It was written to tell the story of how and why the American Constitution emerged as it did. Most books on the history and drafting of the Constitution start with the Revolutionary period. This book explains the influence of the English Revolution and the English constitution on the political values, rights, and liberties of the Revolutionary generation. It also explains why the American Revolution occurred and how its different phases influenced the profound achievement of the Framers in producing their innovative solution for a large and diverse nation.

NOTE

1. "Declaration of Independence" 1776. The Avalon Project, Yale Law School. Accessed November 2018 to July 2020. https://avalon.law.yale.edu/18th_century /declare.asp.

Chapter One

Before the Revolution

The System of Government in America

Why did free Americans turn away from the British system that had created and protected their extraordinary liberties, and risk their new country on what Washington called an "experiment"[1] with a radical new Constitution?

In 1766, Benjamin Franklin had told the British Parliament that until 1763 Americans had seen the British Parliament as "the great bulwark of [Americans'] liberties and privileges."[2] Why did that perception change in the years after 1763?

Americans rebelled when the British threatened what they had enabled—partial American self-government in a system of law and government that enabled free Americans to live independent lives and to enjoy all the opportunities that the colonies and trade with Britain offered.

The Constitution secured the gains of the American Revolution. As America's new fundamental law, it provided for a radical new federal and national system of government and law, built on individual liberty.

Since the British system had made many Americans so free and prosperous, did the new Constitution keep parts of the British system of law and government?

Of course. The objective was to devise and implement an American republican system which would do that—to federalize and republicize the elements of the British system which had produced and protected American liberties. The unique British common law continued in America. The new Courts were based on the British model. The two houses of the new Congress were different from the old Parliament—more like the colonial elected assemblies. But like those assemblies, they had the fundamental character and function of the British House of Commons as chambers of elected representatives who, after debate, would pass the nation's new laws and control taxation and spending by the government. The new office of President was more different from the

British model, but was constrained by Congress and subject to law, as the British Prime Minister was constrained by Parliament and subject to law.

When considering the American Revolutionary period, it is easy to rush to its two most famous achievements—the Declaration of Independence of 1776 and the Constitution of 1787–88. They are radical and inspiring foundational documents of a great country. But to understand both those documents and the system that was established in the United States, it is necessary to have some context.

First, what was the colonial system of government in the thirteen British colonies before they rebelled? What was the basis of their economy and the character of their societies? That is what this chapter is about.

Then, what were the origins of the British system of law and government? The next three chapters tell the story of the British system of government, and Appendix 3 tells how the common law developed.

Then, how did the process of revolutionary constitution making begin in the thirteen colonies? And how were the solutions in the final Constitution developed? Those questions are answered in the final three chapters of this book.

The Constitution of the United States of America was not the first constitution written by the founding generation. It was preceded by the constitutions of eleven States, and the Articles of Confederation. The State constitutions were themselves, in some cases, preceded by colonial charters.

By the time the Framers came to the ultimate Constitution, they had observed how the new State constitutions and the Articles worked in practice. They had refined their analysis of, and solutions to, new problems in political science. They had seen what worked and what did not. They were no longer writing in the excitement and trauma of rebellion, but in the assurance that a new nation had been formed and needed to be protected. They knew that they were designing a new system of government, built on a new foundation—but profoundly influenced by their experience as British subjects living under the British constitution.

The immediate cause of the American Revolution was the British policy in the 1760s and 1770s of trying to increase control over the British colonies in America. British-Americans in the colonies believed that the new laws passed in Britain as part of this policy infringed their rights and liberties under the British constitution and under the arrangements for partial self-government in their colonies. The arrangements for partial self-government are therefore vitally important to an understanding of the American Revolution and the objectives of the revolutionary American Constitution. Those arrangements had their origins in the very beginning, in the founding of the first of the thirteen colonies which rebelled at the time of the Revolution.

THE COLONIAL FOUNDING

The first attempts to establish British colonies in North America occurred during the reign of Elizabeth I. She granted Sir Walter Raleigh a charter to establish a colony. He twice attempted to do that at Roanoke Island, now in North Carolina. The colonists died or went to live with nearby Native Americans.

A British colony was successfully established by a joint stock company at Jamestown, Virginia, in 1607 pursuant to a charter granted by James I in 1606[3]. Virginia had limited self-government. Its General Assembly first convened in 1619 and comprised the members of its Council of State and elected burgesses. Virginia became a Crown colony in 1624, meaning that it came under the direct control of the English monarch. Government was then led by a governor appointed by the king. The Governor was assisted by an appointed Council of State. The General Assembly continued.

Virginia was established as a commercial enterprise. The motivation of the settlers in the next successful colony was not commercial. They were Puritans in search of freedom—especially freedom of worship. The passengers on the Mayflower established their settlement at Plymouth. In November 1620, after they had arrived, they signed the Mayflower Compact[4], a private agreement to cooperate with one another, including in the making of regulations and ordinances which would apply in their new settlement. Plymouth was subject to charters from the time of its establishment until 1774 (except from 1684–91, considered in chapter 2)[5]. From 1629 until 1684, Massachusetts enjoyed almost complete self-government under its own charter of 1629[6]. Connecticut and Rhode Island were later each granted a charter which provided for a similarly high level of self-government. The Massachusetts Charter provided for a "Courte or Assemblie" as a governing body, a "Genarall Courte or Assembly" as a representative body, and an elected Governor.

Both Virginia and Massachusetts began as chartered company colonies, and Virginia became a Crown colony. A third legal model used for the establishment of the thirteen colonies that rebelled in the 1770s was the "proprietary" colony—meaning a colony which was granted to one or more individuals as proprietors, rather than to a special purpose company. The grants of Carolina and Pennsylvania are instructive.

In 1663, the Charter of Carolina[7] (named in honour of Charles I) was granted to the Lords Proprietor—nine men who had helped Charles II in exile or in returning to England and being crowned in 1660. Most of them had received or were to receive new noble titles—including a Dukedom and two Earldoms. The Lords Proprietor were given the power to make laws for the new colony "with the advice, assent and approbation of the freemen of the said province, or of the greater part of them, or of their delegates or deputies." So, there was to be some form of representative assembly involved in the process of making new laws. The Charter allowed for religious freedom for non-Anglican Christians, as the Lords Proprietor were keen to attract immigrants.[8]

The Charter for the Province of Pennsylvania of 1681[9] was far more prescriptive about the Proprietor's lawmaking power. The province was granted to William Penn, a Quaker. Laws made were to be subject to "the advice, assent, and approbation of the Freemen of the said Countrey, or the greater parte of them, or of their Delegates or Deputies." There would be a governor appointed by the Proprietor.

THE SCOPE OF THE POWER
TO MAKE LAWS IN THE COLONIES

Were there limits on the power of the colonial representative assemblies to pass laws? What if an assembly passed a law which was inconsistent with English law or government policy?

Under Virginia's Second Charter of 1609,[10] local laws could be made. They were to be "as near as conveniently may be agreeable to the Laws, Statutes, Government, and Policy of this our Realm of England." A 1621 ordinance of the Company provided that laws and orders approved by majority vote in the General Assembly could be vetoed by the Governor and had to be ratified by the Company in London[11]. That was an attempt by the Company to deal with the risk that the General Assembly might make laws which were inconsistent with English laws in ways which the Company considered were inappropriate. When Virginia became a Crown colony in 1624, its Charter was revoked and not replaced. From that time the risk that the General Assembly might make laws which were inconsistent with English laws was not addressed in a constitutional document.

Under the Massachusetts Charter of 1629, the power to pass laws was express, and the risk that its laws might be inconsistent with English law was addressed. The chartered company had: "full and Absolute Power and Authoritie . . . [to] rule . . . according to the Orders, Lawes, Ordinances, Instructions, and Directions [of the colony], *not being repugnant to the Lawes and Statutes of our Realme of England as aforesaid* [emphasis added]."

If a Massachusettsan law when passed was not repugnant to English law, could the English later pass new laws and claim that colonial laws were repugnant to them? What if the English passed a law which was not inconsistent with a Massachusettsan law, but did infringe a customary freedom? And what if the extension of an English law to the colonies would violate an English constitutional principle, such as "no taxation without representation"? All these unanswered questions became important at the time of the American Revolution.

Carolina's Charter provided that laws had to be "consonant to reason, and as near as may be conveniently, agreeable to the laws and customs of this our kingdom of England" This implied that laws which were repugnant to English laws would not be valid.

Under Pennsylvania's Charter, laws were to be "as neare as conveniently may bee agreeable to the Lawes and Statutes, and rights of this Our Kingdome of England" and court decisions could be appealed to England. A copy of each colonial law of Pennsylvania was to be submitted to the Privy Council in England, and if found to be inconsistent with the Crown's sovereignty or the local lawmaking power, could be struck down as void. Penn was required to keep an agent in London "to Answer for any Misdemeanors that shall be committed, or for any wilfull default or neglect permitted by the said William Penn, his heires or assignee, against our Lawes of Trade or Navigation."

These restrictions in Pennsylvania's Charter of 1681 show that the English wanted that colony to have more constrained rights of self-government than had been granted to some of the older colonies. As we will see in chapter 2, later in the 1680s Kings Charles II and James II took more steps to increase royal control in North America—which provoked a dramatic American response.

By 1776, eight of the thirteen colonies were Crown colonies; three were proprietary; and only two were run by chartered companies[12]. Two of the Crown colonies had charters (Massachusetts and New Hampshire). All the colonies had representative assemblies. Connecticut and Rhode Island each had an elected governor.

Because the British Empire was later so powerful, it is easy to assume that when the colonies were founded England was a rich and powerful country. But the English Crown was not strong or rich enough to establish the colonies, even though the colonies began on a small scale. Companies and individuals, and not the Crown, had to take the enormous risks of founding them. From the beginning, the colonists had local representative government and a political relationship with the English Crown and with Parliament that was different from the relationship of the English in England.

AMERICA IN THE REVOLUTIONARY PERIOD

Fast-forward to the American revolutionary period. How had the colonies fared, and what did the British do to turn the loyal colonists against them?

There are no census data for all thirteen colonies for the pre-revolutionary period. The first census data are from 1790[13]. The U.S. Census Bureau estimates that the total population of the thirteen colonies in 1770 was 2.205 million, and in 1780 was 2.781 million, with a total increase of a massive 41.3 percent in the decade before the 1790 census[14]. At the time of independence, the population was some 0.8 percent of today's population.

Incomes were high. In 1774, the mean income per household per year (in 1774 dollars) in New England was $278, in the middle colonies was $289, and in the southern colonies was $411 if slaves were included and $620 for free whites. This compared with $193 in England and Wales (at an exchange rate of $4.44/£ sterling). Income inequality was much lower in the colonies as well, with a Gini coefficient across the thirteen colonies of 0.40, compared with 0.522 in England and Wales[15].

In New England, farming on small allotments was predominant. Coastal towns engaged in trade. Some 44 percent of households operated farms; 11 percent engaged in professions, commerce, and crafts; and the remainder either did not specify their occupations to the data gatherers or were menial laborers.

In the middle colonies, trade and some manufacturing were important, as well as agriculture. Some 26 percent of households operated farms or plantations; and 33 percent engaged in professions, commerce, and crafts.

In the South, crops grown on plantations, principally for export, were the backbone of the economy. Some 73 percent of free households operated farms or plantations; and 14 percent engaged in professions, commerce, and crafts.

The economic opportunities which had facilitated this prosperity were partly based on the availability of land from which Native Americans had been excluded, and on unfree labour (convicts, indentured servants and, in some colonies, slaves).

The British legal system, applying British and colonial laws, contributed to the colonies' rapid economic development. But one area in which British laws restrained that development was the regulation of trade and shipping—vitally important to the colonies which, although generally prosperous, were much less economically developed than Britain or the Netherlands. The colonists needed to maximize the revenue from their exports and minimize the cost of importing the many goods that they required from Europe.

The "Navigation Act" was passed by the government of the English Republic (or Commonwealth) in 1651 and re-enacted after the re-establishment of the monarchy in England in 1660[16]. It required that goods could be exported only to England, and on colonial or English ships. Imports to the American colonies had to come from English ports. The cargoes on these ships could be subject to English taxes. The new system assured English merchants, manufacturers, ports, ship owners, financiers, and insurers of a preferred position in trade with the colonies. The system of trade and taxation established by the English Republic's Navigation Act became a cornerstone policy and law of the English and then British Empire[17]. It was a momentous development for England's North American Colonies. It featured prominently in the American Revolution.

Under the British governments of Prime Ministers Walpole and Newcastle from 1720 to 1760, the Navigation Act and related legislation were not fully enforced—a policy known as "salutary neglect." The phrase itself is instructive. "Salutary" means bringing health, or beneficial. At least some people in the British Government understood that the laws were not beneficial to the colonies, and that enforcement of them should be neglected.

But instead of repealing the Navigation Act, the British Government reversed its policy of "salutary neglect" in the 1760s, and in several other ways asserted more direct control over the thirteen colonies. The British policy of getting tough on the Americans at that time was the catalyst for the American Revolution.

What led to Britain being more assertive with the colonies?

An immediate cause of the change in policy was the substantial cost of the Seven Years' War of 1754–63 which was largely fought in North America by the British and the colonists against the French and their Native American allies. From the British perspective, it was one thing to allow the British-Americans partial self-government and light taxation[18] when the colonies were inexpensive to administer and provided benefits to Britain under the Navigation Act system. It was another matter when defending those colonies burdened the British Crown and taxpayers with the enormous cost of a major war.

This chapter has sketched the colonial system of government in the thirteen colonies before they rebelled and described how it was a British system with partial self-government. In a later chapter we will look in more detail at the path to rebellion and revolution in America.

The next three chapters will consider how the British system of government had come about, and how the English Revolution led to rebellions in America. The seeds of the American Revolution can be seen in the colonial system of government and in the causes of those rebellions.

NOTES

1. Washington, George. 1789. "First inaugural address as President." The Avalon Project, Yale Law School. Accessed July 2019. https://avalon.law.yale.edu/18th_cen tury/wash1.asp.

2. "Examination of Franklin before the Committee of the Whole of the House of Commons, 13 February 1766." National Archives. Accessed March 2019. https://founders.archives.gov/documents/Franklin/01-13-02-0035.

3. For the text of the foundational documents of the thirteen British colonies that rebelled and formed the United States (from the initial grants or charters up to the time of the American Revolution), an invaluable resource is *Colonial Charters, Grants and Related Documents*. Avalon Project of the Yale Law School Lillian Goldman Law Library. Accessed November 2018 to July 2020. http://avalon.law.yale.edu/subject_menus/statech.asp. This collection includes all the charters for each colony, and other relevant documents such as the 1584 Charter granted by Elizabeth I to Sir Walter Raleigh.

4. "Agreement between the Settlers at New Plymouth, 1620." The Avalon Project, Yale Law School. Accessed March 2019. https://avalon.law.yale.edu/17th_century/mayflower.asp.

5. The charter that established the Virginia Company in 1606 also established the Plymouth Company ("First Charter of Virginia; April 10, 1606." The Avalon Project, Yale Law School. Accessed March to September 2019. https://avalon.law.yale.edu/17th_century/va01.asp.). The Company's shareholders were merchants from Plymouth and other coastal towns in south-west England. The Company founded a colony on the coast of present-day Maine in 1607, but soon abandoned the settlement. The settlers on the Mayflower were authorised by a new charter.

The Charter of New England of 1620 superseded Plymouth's 1606 Charter. Plymouth obtained a new charter in 1629, when Massachusetts Bay formally split from Plymouth and received its own charter.

6. "Charter of Massachusetts Bay, 1691." The Avalon Project, Yale Law School. Accessed March 2019 to July 2020. https://avalon.law.yale.edu/17th_century/mass07.asp.

7. "Charter of Carolina, 1663." The Avalon Project, Yale Law School. Accessed August 2018 to July 2020. https://avalon.law.yale.edu/17th_century/nc01.asp.

8. The treatment of Native Americans by British settlers in the thirteen colonies is beyond the scope of this book. But it is interesting to note differences in the way that founding charters addressed Native Americans. Diseases unwittingly introduced by Europeans, to which the natives had no resistance, had devastated some populations before the colonies were established. The 1620 Charter of New England recited that the area of the grant had been substantially depopulated by disease and conflict among the native inhabitants (perhaps implying that the land rights of the surviving natives did not need to be considered in the Charter). The 1629 Charter of Massachusetts Bay acknowledged that there were natives in Massachusetts and expressed the hope that religious, peaceable, and good government would encourage them to convert to Christianity. The Charter of Carolina in 1663, noted that the land being granted was "only inhabited by some barbarous people, who have no knowledge of Almighty God."

9. "Charter for the Province of Pennsylvania, 1681." The Avalon Project, Yale Law School. Accessed March 2019 to July 2020. https://avalon.law.yale.edu/17th_century/pa01.asp.

10. "Second Charter of Virginia, 1609." The Avalon Project, Yale Law School. Accessed March 2019 to July 2020. https://avalon.law.yale.edu/17th_century/va02.asp.

11. "Ordinance and Constitution of the Treasurer, Council, and Company in England, for a Council of State and General Assembly." 1621. The Avalon Project, Yale Law School. Accessed March to July 2020. https://avalon.law.yale.edu/17th_century/va04.asp.

12. Appendix 1 has a table showing the legal status of each colony when it was established and at the time of independence in 1776.

13. "1790 USA census data." Thomas Jefferson as Secretary of State, viewed at the United States Census Bureau's website. Accessed November 2018 to July 2020. https://www.census.gov/programs-surveys/decennial-census/decade/decennial-publications.1790.html. Appendix 2 has a table showing the 1790 census data.

14. "Population in the Colonial and Continental Periods." The United States Census Bureau. Accessed February 2019 to July 2020. https://www.census.gov/history/pdf/colonialbostonpops.pdf.

15. A Gini coefficient is a statistical measure of dispersion. If everyone had the same income, the Gini coefficient for income distribution would be zero. If one person had all the income, the coefficient would be one. The data in this paragraph come from Lindert, Peter H., and Jeffrey G. Williamson. "American Incomes 1774–1860," *NBER Working Paper No. 18396*, issued in September 2012,. National Bureau of Economic Research's Development of the American Economy programme. Accessed November 29, 2018. https://www.nber.org/papers/w18396.

16. Only three of the thirteen colonies that would rebel against the English in 1776 existed under English law at this time: Virginia, Massachusetts, and Maryland. Settlers in Connecticut, which was part of the Massachusetts Bay Colony, had entered into an agreement amongst themselves known as the "Fundamental Orders" in 1639. Settlement had begun in other areas which later legally became new colonies.

17. Great Britain did not exist as a political entity until England's union with Scotland in 1707. This book generally refers to England before 1707, as Scotland was not involved in colonial affairs or the development of the English constitution before that year.

18. Rabushka, Alvin. 2008. *Taxation in Colonial America*. Princeton University Press.

Chapter Two

The End of Tyranny?

The English Revolution

The American Declaration of Independence of 1776 charged George III with "repeated Injuries and Usurpations, all having in direct Object *the Establishment of an absolute Tyranny* [emphasis added] over these [American] States." In 1649, the English Rump Parliament had charged Charles I with "a wicked design *to erect and uphold in himself an unlimited and tyrannical power to rule* [emphasis added] according to his Will, and to overthrow the Rights and Liberties of the People."[1]

The Founders charged George III with tyranny, rebelled, left his kingdom, and established a republic. The Rump Parliament had charged Charles I with tyranny, tried him, removed his head, and established a republic.

The American republic has endured. The English republic was short-lived. But crucially, the English Civil War and the trial and execution of Charles I had shown the English could overthrow a tyrannous monarchy and replace it with a non-monarchical government. That was a giant step for the prospects of republican government subject to law, and away from government led by a king with divine rights. Charles I's fate was one of the defining events in the long journey to establishing Parliamentary supremacy in England. It is often glossed over or called "regicide" (the murder of a king). The execution was part of the first of the three great rebellions against the English King in the seventeenth and eighteenth centuries. The second was the English or Glorious Revolution of 1688, considered later in this chapter. The third was the American War of Independence and the American Revolution.

Charles was king of England, Scotland, and Ireland. His father was James VI of Scotland who, in 1603, succeeded the great Elizabeth I as James I of England and Ireland. Elizabeth had died without an heir. James had written a book on the divine rights of kings when he was merely king of Scotland (*The True Law of Free Monarchies: or the Reciprocal and Mutual Duty between a*

15

free King and his Natural Subjects[2]). In his book James also emphasized the duties of the monarch, and the monarch's accountability to God.

Charles followed his father's doctrine that kings derive their authority from God and not their subjects. The principle that sovereignty came from the people was not established in the English-speaking world until much later. It was first successfully applied in the constitutions of the newly independent States in America. As we will see, at the time of Charles I's trial it was asserted by the Rump Parliament that the members of the House of Commons as representatives of the people "have the supreme authority in the nation," but that principle was suppressed when the monarchy was restored in 1660.

Most people in James' time were illiterate. Religious practice and belief were pervasive. The fear that gripped England during the demise and death of Elizabeth I was the fear of a war of succession—either a civil war or a foreign invasion. An invasion would have come from one of the great Catholic powers (Spain and France), and may have resulted in attempts to forcibly convert to Catholicism the overwhelmingly Protestant population. People could still remember the burning of Protestants under Elizabeth I's half-sister and predecessor on the throne, Queen Mary.

They were not likely to convert voluntarily to the "Church of Rome." That was the common name in England given to the Roman Catholic Church. The name implied a threat to English independence and freedom. Protestantism and separation from Rome had become important aspects of English national identity.

The horrors of Catholic persecution of Protestants were kept alive from the church pulpit by retelling, and in *Foxe's Book of Martyrs*[3]. That was a huge, illustrated book which graphically told the story of many Christian martyrs, including 300 Protestants killed during the reign of Queen Mary—popularly known as "Bloody Mary" after her death. During her reign, the standard method of executing heretics was burning at the stake. In its first edition in 1563, *Foxe's Book of Martyrs* had run to 1,800 pages and was the weight of a small infant.

The devastating Thirty Years' War in central Europe (1618 to 1648) had begun as a war between Catholic and Protestant states, principally in the Germanic lands.[4] That War also supplied many horrific stories about Protestant deaths and martyrdom.

For James I, the theory of divine right had personal attractions. The murder of a divinely appointed king would be a heinous and monstrous crime. Henry VIII had legally nominated the descendants of his own sister, Mary Tudor, as the successors of his daughter Elizabeth I, in precedence to James' family, the Stuarts. So, James' claim to the throne was contestable. James' father, Henry

Stuart (Lord Darnley) had been murdered. His mother was the notorious Mary Queen of Scots, who was found guilty of high treason and beheaded.

In James' view, the role of Parliament was advisory: decisions could legitimately be made only by the monarch. But, crucially, he learnt to live with Parliament, even when it exceeded what he regarded as its proper role. He passed his divine right doctrine on to his son Charles I.

Charles' 1625 coronation oath in England included that he "[confirmed to the People of England that he would] grant and keep . . . the Laws and Customs to them granted, by the Kings of England . . . agreeable to the Prerogative for the Kings thereof, and the ancient Customs of the Realm."[5] This oath was ambiguous. To a Parliamentarian, the oath included a promise to respect the constitutional aspects of the laws and customs of England, including the role of Parliament in making those laws. But to a king who believed that he was appointed by and accountable to God alone, to promise to "keep . . . the Laws and Customs to [the People of England] granted" was no constraint, because he believed that he could change those laws and customs as he saw fit.

A surprising thing about James' and Charles' belief in the divine right of monarchs is that it was held in the 1600s. The famous "Magna Carta" (or Great Charter) was first issued in 1215[6]—400 years earlier. At that time, the countryside of England was largely controlled by feudal lords and Church institutions. The Charter was forced on King John by some rebel feudal lords or barons and was soon repudiated by John. However, it was reissued on several occasions, including as a statute in 1297[7]. Magna Carta confirmed that the King exercised his powers subject to a legal framework, and was therefore not an absolute monarch but a monarch subject to law. The Charter was not in the form of a contract (which might have implied that the contracting parties had equal status), but a gift or grant. Edward I wrote, when reissuing the Charter in 1297, "freely and out of our good will [had] given and granted to the archbishops, bishops, abbots, priors, earls, barons and all of our realm these liberties written below to hold in our realm of England in perpetuity."[8] This gift or grant was in theory legally enforceable, at least after it became a statute in 1297.

Magna Carta is celebrated most particularly (and especially in the United States) for its assurance of the rights of individual subjects (excluding serfs), including the fundamental right to a writ of habeas corpus—the right to challenge whether a person had been detained or imprisoned lawfully.[9]

Clause 14 of the Charter of 1215 set out the principle that taxes could not be imposed without the consent of an assembly (a forerunner of the modern Parliament), including "archbishops, bishops, abbots, earls and greater barons . . . [and] all who hold in chief of us [i.e., holders of land granted by the Crown]." This was a big step towards "no taxation without representation," which famously became a rallying cry of Britain's American colonies more than 500 years later. It was a principle that Charles I would have been wise to heed.[10]

The proposition that the monarch was subject to law and had to obtain the approval of the monarch's council or of Parliament on at least some issues, such as imposing taxes, seems a more modern doctrine than that monarchs are appointed by and accountable to God alone. How could James I and Charles I assert the divine right of kings so many years after Magna Carta?

Henry VIII's break with the Roman Catholic Church had, in one important way, made it easier for them to do so. The Roman Church saw itself as the intermediary between God and monarchs. Whether a monarch was appointed by God or continued to enjoy God's confidence was a question determined by the Pope.

Henry VIII established a Church of England free from Papal authority. Because James did not need to acknowledge that the Pope or Church stood between him and God, and after the strong Tudor monarchs, James' theory of the divine right of monarchs was more credible in the early seventeenth century than it would have been before the Tudors and the break with Rome.

The chaos and devastation of the European Thirty Years War also helped the case for stable government with established legitimacy—inherited monarchs appointed by God. That War was ultimately settled by the perpetuation of most pre-War rulers' power.

In other ways though, the assertion of a theory of divine right was less credible during Charles I's reign than it would have been at the time of Magna Carta. While Henry VIII's break with Rome met his immediate needs, it had the downside of promoting Protestant belief. That belief disintermediated the relationship between the King's subjects and God. Protestant teaching, especially that of Martin Luther, emphasized a direct and personal relationship between each Christian and God. The Church could facilitate this relationship but did not broker or intermediate it.

By Charles I's time, England's economic and political life were no longer organized on feudal principles. The Kingdom had seen off an invasion attempt by the European superpower of the day, Spain, in 1588. The Church of England had developed a narrative of its own legitimacy which did not include any dependence on the Pope. Authority in, and decisions about, doctrine in the Church of England were distinctly English, independent of any authority or power on the European continent.

So, while the establishment of the Church of England meant that the kings of England were not subject to the Pope's authority, it also meant that the king's subjects were less likely to regard the Church or its ministers as the sole interpreters of God's will.

This was even more true of members of those Protestant denominations which were more radical than the Church of England, the "nonconformists" or Puritans, who were prominent among those who challenged Charles I. And prominent among those who abandoned England to establish a new Godly society in New England.

Foreseeing a risk to its role as the monopoly intermediator with God, the Church of Rome had tried to suppress English language bibles. But illegal English language bibles had still circulated. Henry VIII had in 1539 authorized the use of an English language bible in the new Church of England (the "Great Bible").

By the time of James I's reign, several English language translations were in use, and James decided that it would be better to have a translation in general use that was acceptable to him and the Church of England. In 1604 he initiated the translation project. In 1611 the English language "King James Version" of the bible was published. The translation drew on primary non-English sources, as well as earlier English translations, in particular that of William Tyndale. The King James Version is a beautiful work of literature, as well as being a holy book. It was intended to be read aloud, and its rhythms and cadences are compelling. As the one book known well by most Protestants in the English-speaking world for the next 350 years, it is a bedrock of English-language literary culture.[11]

The English language bibles, in particular the King James Version, not only made the word of God more immediate and accessible for most of the population (who could not read or speak Latin) but were a phenomenal accelerator of literacy—which rose from some 5 percent of the population in 1500 to some 53 percent by 1650. The newly literate were both less dependent on their priests and easier to reach by printed propaganda and polemics[12].

Population growth and economic development, while slow by the standards of the nineteenth and twentieth centuries, had accelerated in England during the sixteenth century. The data are not perfect, but one authoritative study puts the population of England and Wales at 2,642,000 in 1500 and 4,470,000 in 1600[13], and GDP per capita (in 1990 US dollars) at 793 in 1500 and 1,080 in 1600—a significant increase on a per capita basis, and a huge increase for that era on an aggregate basis. The increase was driven by increased trade and urbanization (from 3.1 percent of the population in 1500 to 13.3 percent in 1600), as well as improvements in the productivity of agriculture.[14] Some of the newly wealthy were independently minded and pious Protestants, including Puritans.

As for trade, improvements in shipping and navigation technology, as well as the success of Francis Drake and others in finding wealth in the Atlantic (through trade, but also as privateers, plundering Spanish shipping), led to an explosion of English shipping activity. A partial national survey in 1560 listed 76 merchant ships of 100 tons or more. A more comprehensive survey in 1582 found 178 ships of that size. Between 1589 and 1610, a further 384 ships of that size were built in England[15].

The first royal charter for the occupation of land in what became the United States of America was granted to Walter Raleigh in 1584. He named the place Virginia in honor of the virgin queen, Elizabeth. In 1600, the famous East India Company, which later came to govern much of what are now India, Pakistan, and Bangladesh, was established by royal charter.

So, when Charles I ascended the throne in 1625, his Kingdom was a dynamic nation. The nation had ancient liberties, no control by foreigners, increasing prosperity, successful entrepreneurs, higher literacy rates, more free-thinking people, increasing interaction with the rest of the world, and increased self-confidence.

From early in his reign, Charles had a tumultuous relationship with Parliament. In 1628, Parliament adopted a Petition of Right,[16] after Charles had sought to impose taxes without the consent of Parliament and had imprisoned some of his subjects who had refused to pay his illegal taxes.

The Petition of Right, in the form of a declaration and not a statute, covered some of the same issues as Magna Carta. It provided that there should be no taxation without the consent of Parliament, no forced billeting of soldiers, and no unlawful imprisonment. As a petition, it was not clear that it had binding legal status, even when the King accepted its terms. But as a statement of position and intent by Parliament, it was a forceful assertion of the liberties of the English and the limits on the power of their government.

The process of raising revenue without Parliament's consent not only produced a response from Parliament, it also earnt Charles the hostility of many powerful people in his Kingdom. His revenue raising activities included:

- fining knights who had not attended his coronation;
- raising "ship money," a tax on certain ports and coastal areas;
- selling the rights to monopolies in various products;
- revoking certain land grants in Scotland;
- seizing land by reasserting the ancient boundaries of royal forests;
- seizing private silver held in the Tower of London (but promising to later return it, with interest); and
- seizing stocks of the East India Company (and then selling them below market value, and promising to repay the amount received, plus interest).

In 1629, the King recalled Parliament and asked it to approve more taxes. Instead, the House of Commons proposed and debated three extraordinary resolutions.[17] The first was a resolution that any person who sought to introduce Popish changes in religious practice would commit a capital offence. This was a response to Archbishop Laud's attempts, supported by Charles, to move the worship of the Church of England closer to the Catholic model. Charles' wife was Catholic, and he had sought to restrain non-conformists, so his government was not trusted on religious issues by the members of the fiercely Protestant Commons.

The second resolution attacked the King's ministers and advisers, by providing that it would be a capital offence to counsel or advise any taxation without the approval of Parliament. A capital offence is one punishable by death. It would have been treasonous to articulate a circumstance in which the King could be decapitated. But the law against treason did not protect his ministers and advisers.

The third resolution provided that any person who paid such a tax would be "a betrayer of the liberties of England, and an enemy of the same." Just what the consequence of being a betrayer or enemy would be was not stated. Perhaps that was because the Commons was a bit rushed in its debate on the resolutions. The Speaker of the House tried to terminate the debate by rising from his chair, but he was forcibly held down to prevent this, and the King's soldiers were beating on the locked doors of the Commons' chamber trying to terminate the Commons' proceedings.

Eight days later, Charles dissolved Parliament. After a further thirteen years, the catastrophe of an English civil war began (war against the Scots came sooner).

War led to the arrest and trial of Charles, who had insisted on his divine rights and failed to understand that it was imperative for him to allow Parliament its rights—both because they were long established legal and customary rights and because Parliament reflected the opinions and sentiments of that part of the English population which had local authority in the kingdom and expected to have some say in the country's affairs.

After Charles' trial and execution, there was a period of republican government without a monarch—the Commonwealth (1649–1653), and then the Protectorate (1653–1659).

There were many important events in this tumultuous period. This book cannot deal with them in detail. What follows is a short summary of the events that led to the King's trial. The period merits further reading. It is unfortunate that many people in the English-speaking countries know more about the French Revolution than they do about the trial and execution of an English king and the short-lived first English republic[18]. The English civil wars and first English republic led indirectly to the enhancement of the power of Parliament and the curbing of the monarchy—significant steps towards freedom and political representation for the people of England; and a vital catalyst to the system of government adopted by the United States of America when the thirteen colonies broke with Britain in the next century. This left Britain and America with the most pluralistic political institutions in the world. These pluralistic political institutions facilitated technological and economic innovation, and prosperity.

War began in 1639 after Charles tried to impose on the Scottish church (the "Kirk") some Anglican practices of worship, which included modified versions of Catholic rituals. The Kirk in Scotland was more radically Protestant than the Church of England. Charles did not initially engage the Scottish rebel army in battle. He convened a Parliament seeking more funds. Many of the members of the House of Commons elected to this Parliament were not favorably disposed to the King and were not inclined to grant him funds for a war against the Scots. Charles prorogued the Parliament in May 1640, less than a month after it had assembled. This Parliament is known as the Short Parliament.

While Charles was the King of each of England, Wales, Scotland, and Ireland, each of Scotland and Ireland had its own parliament and government. The Scottish Parliament declared that it would govern without the King's consent. The Scots invaded northern England.

Still needing funds, in November 1640 Charles summoned another English Parliament—later known as the Long Parliament—because there was no election for another Parliament until 1660[19]. In 1640 and 1641, this Parliament impeached several of the King's key advisers, passed an Act requiring that Parliament must convene at least once every three years, and another Act which provided that Parliament could not be dissolved without its own consent.[20]

In January 1642, Charles illegally invaded the House of Commons with an armed guard to arrest five members on the grounds of high treason. They were forewarned and got away by boat (on the Thames River, which was adjacent to the Commons' chamber). Charles had committed an extreme breach of Parliamentary privilege, appeared incompetent, and further lost royal prestige.

Parliament seized London. Charles fled. He sent his wife and one of his children abroad for safety. The first battle of the English Civil War took place at Edgehill on October 23, 1642. War between the King and Parliament ended with the victory of Parliament's New Model Army over the Royalists and their allies at the Battle of Preston in August 1648. Another civil war was to follow Charles' death, with the royalists led by his elder son, the future Charles II.[21]

After Parliament's victory, most members of Parliament still favored negotiation with the King. The Army was more radical. In December 1648, the
Army illegally purged Parliament of members who favored negotiation—it
became the "Rump Parliament." This Rump purported to indict Charles on
a charge of high treason, and to establish a court to try him. On January 4,
1649, the Rump Parliament purported to give itself the power to make laws,
by a declaration which included that "the Commons of England assembled in
Parliament, being chosen by and representing the people, *have the supreme
authority of the nation* [emphasis added]." [22]

The sovereignty of the citizens had been a concept of political philosophy
known since the days of Ancient Athens and had been applied by the leading
Protestant country of the day, the Dutch Republic. At that time, the Dutch Republic was the most prosperous state in the world, and the most modern. The
Dutch declaration of independence, the "Act of Abjuration" of 1581, had not
used the language of 'supreme authority' or sovereignty, but it had asserted
the right of subjects to remove and replace a prince:

> And when [a prince who is the ruler of a people] . . . oppresses them, seeking op-
> portunities to infringe their ancient customs and privileges, exacting from them
> slavish compliance, then he is no longer a prince, but a tyrant, *and the subjects
> are to consider him in no other view. And . . . they may not only disallow his
> authority, but legally proceed to the choice of another prince for their defense*
> [emphasis added]. [23]

THE TRIAL OF CHARLES I

Was Charles' trial legal? Or was it just a spurious attempt to legitimize the
proposed murder of the King?

Because the Court that tried Charles was established by an Act [24] of the
Rump Parliament, the Court and trial were not authorized in accordance with
the English constitution as it existed before and after the English republic. If
the republic is not regarded as lawful, then the trial was not lawful. But if the
revolutionary republic is accepted as the sole and legitimate government of
England at the time, notwithstanding its revolutionary origins, then the trial
was lawful. History has favored the restoration of the monarchy, and the view
that the republic and its actions were an illegal aberration. [25]

The King was not tortured, he heard the charge against him, and he was
given the opportunity to address the Court and defend himself. [26] All these
processes adopted by the Court were fairer to the accused than was usual in
treason trials in that period.

Even though later monarchs cast all aspects of the trial as illegal and treasonous, the fact that the King had been executed by his subjects was a startling reminder to any subsequent King or Queen of England who was frustrated by the limits on his or her power. Charles' fate was a giant step towards the current system of government in the United Kingdom. That system is a republic disguised as a monarchy (discussed in chapter 4).

The basis of the charge against Charles is the beginning of the legal doctrine that a ruler is not immune from prosecution and can be tried for crimes against his or her subjects—a forerunner of the modern charge of "crimes against humanity."[27]

The Articles of Impeachment of Charles[28] described him as plain "Charles Stuart . . . admitted King of England." The charge described him as having limited powers, subject to law. It said that he was "obliged to use the power committed to him for the good and benefit of the people, and for the preservation of their rights and liberties." He had breached his coronation oath and "[acted to] overthrow the rights and liberties of the people . . . which by the fundamental constitutions of this kingdom were reserved on the people's behalf in the right and power of frequent and successive Parliaments . . ."

In particular, he had committed treason by making war against the Parliament and the people therein represented. As the instigator of those wars, he was guilty of all "the treasons, murders, rapines, burnings, spoils, desolations, damages and mischiefs to this nation, acted and committed [by the Royalist forces in those wars] . . ."

No mention was made of Charles having been appointed by God. Even more striking was the charge of treason. The law of treason normally protected the monarch. Now it was used against the delinquent Charles to protect the Parliament and the people as the alleged supreme source of legal authority in England, at least when the monarch was in breach of the constitution and had pursued "a wicked design to erect and uphold in himself an unlimited and tyrannical power to rule according to his Will." (As noted at the beginning of this chapter, the Declaration of Independence in 1776 would charge George III with having an objective of establishing tyranny over the colonies.).

Putting aside the question of whether the Court was legally constituted, how legal were the charges? To what extent were they based on new notions which had no basis in law, and were merely invented by the lawyers for the prosecution, led by the Solicitor-General, John Cooke?

If Charles had breached his coronation oath and the constitution, he had acted unlawfully. Whether he had committed treason and was subject to capital punishment is less clear. Sources such as Magna Carta and the coronation oath had not dwelt on what would happen to a monarch who breached them. Cooke and his team presumably reasoned that breach of such fundamental constitutional documents could not be mere breaches of promises or contract. If they were violations which amounted to breach of a fundamental duty to and betrayal of the kingdom, they were at least analogous to treason. And if it were the sovereign who had committed this betrayal, he could surely not remain the sovereign.

Charles declined to recognize the jurisdiction of the Court over him. His failure to plead meant that, at common law as it then stood, he was taken to have confessed.

After the restoration of Charles' son, as Charles II, some of the leading players in his trial, including the great John Cooke, were quickly tried and executed.

What is important to this book is not so much the dramatic story of Charles I's demise, but the way that the whole affair ultimately helped to advance the English constitution from being centred on a monarch appointed by God, towards Parliament having the central role in the constitution, and towards the people being the source of ultimate authority or sovereignty[29].

Charles I was executed on January 30, 1649. Charles II (as he was about to become) returned from exile on May 29, 1660. These eleven years are often called "the interregnum," or the period between kings. That is the royalist perspective. For republicans, they were eleven years where government was successfully conducted without a hereditary monarch. Because the republican government has generally been treated as an illegal aberration, the period is usually not characterized as part of the legal progression in England towards the pre-eminence of the House of Commons and the sovereignty of the people.

Yet it is one of the defining events of the history of England, and in particular of English government. The uncertain legality of the Rump Parliament's proceedings cannot obscure the stupendous significance of a proud King being tried for tyranny, and John Cooke staring him down and making him subject to the law.

Both the fact that Charles I was executed (whether it was legal or not), and the fact that there was vigorous government for eleven years without a monarch, have helped to constrain English monarchs ever since from acting unconstitutionally. The one reckless exception was Charles I's second son, James II, and things did not go well for him, as we shall see.

A Note on Terminology

A civil war followed by the trial of a king and the establishment of a republic would meet most definitions of a revolution, and these events in England in the 1640s are sometimes called "the English Revolution." But that phrase is not in general use for those events, so it is not used in this book.

The events in 1688–89 at the end of and after James II's reign, considered later in this chapter, are often called "the Glorious Revolution" and sometimes called "the English Revolution." Some historians have described the period from the beginning of the English Civil War until the mid-1690s as a revolutionary period.

In this book, "the Glorious Revolution" and "the English Revolution" are used interchangeably to describe the events of 1688–89. The former phrase has been used because it is often used and the latter has been used because, in my view, it is better. This Revolution was arguably the first momentous modern European revolution,[30] and giving it a triumphalist descriptor which does not even identify where it occurred is not helpful when assessing its significance against other revolutions.

The Commonwealth and Protectorate period advanced the political power and expectations of classes of people who were gaining increased economic power and who were not sympathetic to arbitrary royal power or the land-owning aristocracy, including merchants, manufacturers, and entrepreneurial agriculturalists. The subsequent reigns of Charles II and James II thwarted that political power and those expectations. But James II's reign was cut short, and the English Revolution permanently ended arbitrary royal power.

In the republic (known as the Commonwealth of England) established after the execution of Charles I, the executive functions of government were first exercised by a Council of State. The office of king was abolished. So was the House of Lords. There were no fresh elections, but some of the members of the House of Commons who had been purged were readmitted—so the Commons became more than a rump, and less committed to the most radical views of the Puritans and the New Model Army.

Oliver Cromwell is the most famous figure of the Commonwealth and the subsequent Protectorate. A puritan member of the House of Commons, he had emerged as an outstandingly successful military leader during the civil wars. He was a cavalry officer. He had great success in training and motivating his men, as well as introducing close-order cavalry formations and successfully maintaining his battle formations on the field so that they did not disintegrate after the initial charge.

He led an army to Ireland in 1649–50, a campaign which still lives in infamy in Irish memory. Whether he slaughtered civilians to an extent that exceeded common practice at the time, as is generally remembered in Ireland, is uncertain. The campaign was conducted to avenge Catholic atrocities against Protestants in Ireland in 1641 and to suppress Catholicism, as well as to establish Commonwealth control over Ireland, where support for Charles I had been strong.

The campaign continued for almost three years after Cromwell ceased to lead it. The appalling number of deaths occurred largely during the guerrilla phase of the fighting, after Cromwell had left Ireland. In response to attacks on English supply lines, the Commonwealth destroyed food supplies and evicted civilians. Famine followed, and then bubonic plague.

In February 1649, the Scottish Parliament had proclaimed Charles II as king of "Great Britain, France and Ireland." In 1650, Cromwell left Ireland for Scotland. He had another brilliant victory, at Dunbar. He then pursued Charles' army into England and defeated it at the Battle of Worcester. Charles just managed to escape by hiding in forests and in the priest holes of several Catholic houses. He fled to France and then to the Netherlands.

In 1653, Cromwell dissolved the expanded Rump Parliament by force. It was replaced by a Nominated Assembly (derisively called by Royalists the "Barebones Parliament," after one of its members named Praise-God Barebones). This was the end of the Commonwealth and beginning of the "Protectorate."

The "Instrument of Government," England's first written constitution, was adopted in December 1653.[31] It provided for a Head of State and head of the executive Government, styled the "Lord Protector." Cromwell was the initial Lord Protector, for life. After his death, the Protector was to be chosen by Council. The Lord Protector had a right to be consulted about the terms of new legislation, but not to veto it. The Lord Protector was to be assisted in executive government by a Council, whose initial members were specified and whose subsequent members were to be selected by Parliament.

The county franchise for voting in elections of members of Parliament was set at any property to a value of at least two hundred pounds. The borough franchise was determined by the boroughs. Catholics were disqualified from voting or election. Royalists were not eligible to vote or be elected for the next four triennial parliaments. Irish Royalists were barred for life.

The great offices of Chancellor, Keeper or Commissioners of the Great Seal, the Treasurer, Admiral, Chief Governors of Ireland and Scotland, and the Chief Justices of both the Benches were retained, and the holders of these offices were to be appointed by Parliament. There was to be a standing army of 20,000 foot-soldiers and 10,000 cavalry.

Freedom of religion was assured to Christian sects "provided this liberty be not extended to Popery or Prelacy, nor to such as, under the profession of Christ, hold forth and practise licentiousness." The reference to licentiousness was perhaps prompted by the existence of the Ranters, a sect whose members were generally believed to eschew all authority and law, and to celebrate nudity and liberal sexual practices.

In short, despite many successes, including in foreign policy, the Commonwealth and the Protectorate were doomed by their reliance on Puritans and on Puritan sentiment in the New Model Army. From its origins in the Army's purge of Parliament in December 1648, the Commonwealth had not fairly represented the people of England, or even English men who owned property. The Rump Parliament and then the National Assembly were dominated by a Puritan minority.

After the civil wars and the novelty of Puritan republican government, familiarity and moderation were alluring. As the Protectorate became less stable and popular, royalists, conservatives and opportunists all began to see the restoration of the Stuarts as an attractive alternative. Charles, son of Charles I, faced little opposition when he returned from exile. He was crowned on April 23, 1661.

THE RESTORATION OF STUART KINGS

The reign of Charles II began with the vengeful show trials of several men involved in the trial and execution of the now sainted martyr, Charles I. Twelve of them were hanged, drawn, and quartered. One was beheaded. Others were imprisoned for life. Some were pardoned. Some who had died before the restoration (including Cromwell, and the president of the Court that had tried and sentenced Charles I, John Bradshaw) had their bodies dug up and "executed."

The Kingdom was happy to enjoy a period of respite from the horrors of the civil war and the stresses of republican rule by Puritans. Charles II enjoyed his pleasures and indulgences. He had no children by his wife but recognized twelve children from seven mistresses. Theatres, closed by the Puritans, reopened under Charles. Anglicanism resumed its dominance over other Protestant sects.

The restoration of the monarchy led to a vigorous period of acquiring and establishing new English colonies in North America. Connecticut became a chartered colony in 1662. As noted in chapter 1, Carolina was granted to nine supporters of Charles II as a proprietary colony in 1663. Rhode Island was given its own charter in the same year.[32] The New Netherlands (later New York, New Jersey, and Delaware) was granted to the Duke of York (Charles II's bother, the future James II) in 1664. The Dutch had surrendered it to a fleet representing the Duke.

But in both the established and new colonies, the colonists' understanding of their constitutional rights and status was different from the understanding of both Charles and his brother James. The colonists saw themselves as having the rights of Englishmen, adapted to their overseas locations. These included rights to elected local legislatures, with the Crown having only the right to review laws passed by these legislatures. They believed that their rights extended to no taxation without the consent of the local legislature, except for customs on goods sent to England. The King and the proprietors (the most significant of whom was the Duke of York) did not accept this model. The King resisted attempts by Virginians in 1675 to adopt a charter which would have legally conferred such rights on the colonists. Massachusetts's sainted Charter of 1629 was revoked in 1684. New York's attempts to gain a charter were unsuccessful.[33]

In the Crown colonies, Charles II saw the system of government as a matter for him to determine using his royal 'prerogative powers' (residual powers of the monarch which were not subject to approval by Parliament or review by the Courts). The proprietary colonies should be governed by the proprietors, subject to any rights of the colonists provided for in the grants to the proprietors.

In both England and America, there was some popular apprehension about Charles having married a Catholic Portuguese princess. There was more concern about the prospect of his successor—his brother James, the Duke of York, a Catholic. However, James' first wife was an Anglican and his two daughters with her, Mary and Anne, were brought up as Anglicans. Mary, the elder daughter, married the Protestant Dutch ruler Prince William of Orange[34].

Religious issues remained prominent during Charles II's reign. In 1662, an "Act of Uniformity" was passed to prohibit Puritan practices in parts of the Church of England, by making compulsory the use of the *Book of Common Prayer*. The "Test Act" of 1673 in effect excluded Catholics from any civil or military office except membership of the House of Lords. Under that Act, it was necessary to swear that transubstantiation did not occur when bread and wine were offered to worshippers during Holy Communion. This was a reference to the Catholic belief that the bread and wine given to worshipers during the ceremony of Holy Communion became the body and blood of Christ (hence, changing into a different substance), while Protestants believed that they merely symbolized the body and blood of Christ. In 1678, the Test Act was extended to membership of the House of Lords.

In 1679, the House of Commons proposed an Exclusion Bill which, if passed into law, would have excluded Charles' brother James from succeeding to the throne because he was a Catholic. Early in 1681, Charles dissolved Parliament to ensure that the Bill did not become law. Charles is said to have converted to Catholicism on his deathbed. James succeeded to the throne in 1685.

James II would have been wise to keep his Catholicism to himself, to avoid reviving the specters of Catholic persecution of Protestants and of the possibility of invasion by one of the Catholic powers of Europe. He did not.

He would have been wise to offer no repeat of his father's defiance of Parliament, which led to the horrors of civil war. He did not.

And if by his second wife (a Catholic) he had a son (who would leapfrog Mary and Anne as successor to the throne), James would have been wise to bring him up as a Protestant. He did not.

Such astonishing disregard for the sentiments of his subjects had unsurprising consequences for James. He was not king for long.

For England, James' demise was the catalyst for a settlement that stabilized relations between Catholics and Protestants, and clarified relations between the monarch and Parliament. This had profound consequences for England, and for the world. Over the following centuries, social and economic development empowered businesspeople and townspeople. There was no subsequent civil war or revolution in England[35]. Instead, the new arrangements allowed a slow but continuous adaptation of government to changed social and economic conditions. The changes of 1688 were at the heart of the momentous English Revolution.

Both James I and Charles II had Catholic sympathies but understood that displaying or promoting them would be traumatic for many of their subjects. James I objected fundamentally to Parliament's authority but accommodated himself to it. James II had his father Charles I's inflexibility in dealing with Parliament and an insensitivity on the fundamental issue of religious alignment, that are quite astonishing in view of the then recent history of his Kingdom.

Before the New Model Army, there had been no professional standing army in England. Because England was on an island, it was not subject to the constant threat of invasion by a large foreign army. Its geography allowed the English to raise armies only when needed, rather than having a standing force that would be expensive to keep and could be used to impose tyranny on England itself. The absence of a standing army, which could have been used by English kings to suppress their subjects, was a constraint on English kings' power. The New Model Army had been disbanded when Charles II became king, but its effectiveness could not be forgotten.

Charles II had established a small standing army, including troops from the New Model Army. James II greatly increased the size of the army and billeted many of his unruly soldiers in private premises throughout England. He had Catholics installed as senior officers, alleging that he had a prerogative right to do so, even though this was prohibited by an Act of Parliament. He dismissed judges who were not sympathetic to his views. He tried to stack local government bodies with people on whom he could rely. He embarked on a massive program of Catholicizing and modernizing England, using Louis XIV's France as his model[36]. When Parliament objected to these alarming innovations, James prorogued[37] Parliament, which did not meet again during his reign.

In North America, James went further than his brother Charles II in asserting direct royal power. In 1686 he established the Dominion of New England, which swallowed up all the colonies of New England. In 1688, New York and New Jersey were added to the Dominion. Being incorporated into a new, consolidated royal colony in 1686 was especially traumatic for the Puritans of Massachusetts and Connecticut. They had been accustomed to a high degree of independence in their government, protected by their Charters. For them, the purpose of their colonies was not only to protect their property from royal predation, including taxation without consent. It was most fundamentally about living under a government led by and for Puritans, a holy commonwealth.

In 1686 James further inflamed Protestant fears by publishing two papers written by the late Charles II, arguing why Catholicism should be preferred to Protestantism. Charles' arguments included that there was one Church, which derived its authority directly from Jesus Christ via his apostles, and that it was anathema for ordinary people to think that they could interpret scripture[38]. James' publication included a paper by his late first wife, the Anglican Anne Hyde, pleading for tolerance towards Catholics.

James II received a Papal nuncio, or ambassador, at Court. James was the first English monarch to do that since Bloody Mary. He began to purge Anglican holders of high civil offices, and to replace them with Catholics, notwithstanding the Test Act. This aggravated the aristocrats who lost their positions and attendant incomes. In 1687 he issued the Declaration of Indulgence[39], seeking to override laws which discriminated against Catholics and radical Protestants.

The Declaration purported to override the Test Act, but then acknowledged that Parliament perhaps should have a role in such matters: "We therefore . . . have thought fit by virtue of our royal prerogative to issue forth this our declaration of indulgence, making no doubt of the concurrence of our two Houses of Parliament *when we shall think it convenient for them to meet* [emphasis added]."

This was bizarre. James had suspended Parliament for not agreeing with his policies. But his Declaration stated that he had no doubt that Parliament would concur with the repeal of the Test Act. That implausible presumption was presented as a substitute for actual Parliamentary approval. The Declaration acknowledged the necessity of Parliamentary approval of the repeal of a statute but then asserted a right for the King to unilaterally repeal Parliament's legislation.

The King stated in the Declaration that he heartily wished "that all the people of our dominions were members of the Catholic Church." This statement was no doubt intended to disarm critics, who would suspect that his declaration of religious tolerance was primarily about freeing Catholics from their constraints, so that he could promote and prefer them. He came straight out and admitted his preference for Catholicism. But it was an odd thing to try to appear tolerant by acknowledging a personal preference for the Church of Rome holding a religious monopoly in England. Not only would transition to such a monopoly bring devastating deaths and persecution, but it would also require most of his subjects outside of Ireland to abandon their most cherished beliefs and, according to those beliefs, be condemned to Hell.

The Declaration was not even kept quiet. In 1688 James ordered that it be read from every Anglican pulpit. It is quite astonishing that the fourth Stuart king issued a document that neatly demonstrated the Stuarts' contempt for Parliament and yearning for the Catholic Church—the two most perilous issues for the Stuarts since the accession of James I, way back in 1603. The Stuarts had surely had enough time to learn. Now, time was nearly up.

Seven bishops, including the most senior Anglican bishop (the Archbishop of Canterbury), petitioned for the reconsideration of the King's religious policies. They were arrested and tried for sedition.

Then James' Catholic wife, Princess Mary of Modena, gave birth to a son, James, displacing the Anglican Mary and Anne in the order of succession. The overwhelmingly Protestant population of England was faced with the prospect that James' elevation of papists and promotion of the Church of Rome would not end with him—it could become permanent.

THE ENGLISH REVOLUTION

In June 1688, seven Protestants wrote to Prince William of Orange, inviting him to come to England. The seven were the Earl of Shrewsbury, the Earl of Danby, the Viscount Lumley, the Bishop of London, Admiral Edward Russell, and Henry Sidney.[40] The letter was remarkably balanced. It pleaded for William's intervention, advising him that:

- "the people are so generally dissatisfied with the present conduct of the government in relation to their religion, liberties and properties (all which have been greatly invaded), and they are in such expectation of their prospects being daily worse, that your Highness may be assured there are

nineteen parts of twenty of the people throughout the kingdom who are de-
sirous of a change, and who, we believe, would willingly contribute to it.";
- "not one in a thousand here believes [the infant James] to be the Queen's
  [child].";
- many aristocrats were likely to support an invasion by William; and
- James II was likely to find the army unreliable ("we do upon very good
  grounds believe that their army then would be very much divided among
  themselves, many of the officers being so discontented that they continue
  in their service only for a subsistence . . . and very many of the common
  soldiers do daily shew such an aversion to the popish religion that there
  is the greatest probability imaginable of great numbers of deserters which
  would come from them should there be such an occasion").

But the letter also warned that it had not been possible for the conspirators
to obtain many firm commitments of support for the plan, and that intelligence of William's preparations might forearm James. The possibility that
Louis XIV would intervene to support his cousin and co-religionist, James
II, was not mentioned. (Much of William's career had been spent saving the
Dutch Republic from invasions by the rapacious French Sun King. For William, James' attempts to Catholicize England raised the possibility of a later
alliance between France and England, which may have been fatal for the
Dutch Republic.)

William and his army landed in Tor Bay, in Devon, on November 5, 1688.
A site so far west of London was chosen to allow time for English supporters to gather before James could deploy his army to oppose the invaders. On
landing, William issued a declaration of the "reasons inducing him to appear
in arms in the Kingdom of England, and for preserving the Protestant religion,
and for restoring the laws and liberties of England, Scotland, and Ireland."[41]

His army was considerable: including some 7,600 foot soldiers and some
3,600 dragoons and cavalry. About half of them were British. William had
received substantial financial aid from some of James' subjects. William
brought arms for some 20,000 English supporters.

James' force was initially larger, although less experienced. Louis XIV
sent James money, but James declined the French despot's offer of military
support, concerned that accepting soldiers from the Catholic monarch would
further alienate his subjects.

On November 9, William took Exeter. From November 12, nobles began
to declare their support for William. On November 19, James joined his army
at Salisbury.

There were rebellions against James throughout England, Scotland, and
Wales. Many Protestant officers deserted James. On November 24, General

Churchill, one of James' most senior officers, deserted. (He was the son of a Sir Winston Churchill and forbear of the twentieth-century British Prime Minister Sir Winston Churchill.) General Churchill left a letter for James: "I hope the great advantage I enjoy under Your Majesty, which I own I would never expect in any other change of government, may reasonably convince Your Majesty and the world that I am actuated by a higher principle . . ."[42]

If this statement was sincere, it was a neat summary of the effect of James' Catholic policies, even for those of his loyal subjects who had benefitted during his reign. On November 26, James became aware that his daughter Anne had deserted him for William and William's wife Mary (Anne's sister).

James feared that his army was unreliable and was reluctant to engage in battle. The minor Battle of Reading on December 9 was the biggest encounter, leaving some twenty to fifty Royalists dead, and a few Dutch dead.

James was allowed to flee to France on his second attempt—the first time, he was caught near Faversham by some fishermen and brought back to London. On his way across the Thames, he famously threw the Great Seal of the Realm into the river. James' departure was an excellent outcome for William: James had vacated the throne and abandoned his country, but not been martyred in the process.

William did not claim the throne. He was invited to head a provisional Government. An elected Convention Parliament met on January 22, 1689. It was divided into Commons and Lords, but not called a Parliament because the writs for a new Parliament could be issued only by a monarch.

A letter from William was read: it mixed deference to the Convention Parliament with a reminder of what had recently been achieved (without directly taking credit for it), and a statement that the Dutch States may soon require the return of their military forces, so that "next to the Danger of unseasonable Divisions amongst yourselves, nothing can be so fatal as too great Delay in your Consultations . . ."[43] It was a well-crafted letter. William's experience in dealing with the Dutch States and their republic had prepared him well for dealing with the English.

The Convention Parliament declared a day of thanksgiving "to Almighty God, for having made His Highness the Prince of Orange the glorious Instrument of the great Deliverance of this Kingdom from Popery and Arbitrary Power . . ."[44]

On January 28, the Commons resolved that James had "endeavoured to subvert the Constitution of this Kingdom, by breaking the Original Contract between King and People; and, by the Advice of Jesuits, and other wicked Persons, having violated the fundamental Laws."[45] Note the reference to a contract between a monarch and his or her subjects. This was an echo of the charges against Charles I, and a recognition of the "People" as a political entity with whom the King had contracted. The concept of "fundamental laws" (often called natural law) was stated as a second legal constraint on the King's conduct.

The sanction against James for these breaches did not need to be determined, because he had already "withdrawn himself out of the Kingdom; . . . abdicated the Government; and . . . the Throne is thereby vacant . . ."

The resolution was adopted by the whole of the Convention Parliament on February 6. On February 13, William and Mary were offered the throne. Mary was James II's eldest child, and James II was William's uncle and father-in-law, but the invitation did not mention any claim to the throne under normal rules of succession. Any such statement would have been legally and politically contentious because James II's infant son James was the heir-apparent to the throne under normal principles of succession.

The invitation noted both William's role in delivering the Kingdom from Popery and arbitrary power, and his virtues. It then went on to invite William and Mary to accept the Crown on the authority of the Lords and Commons. This was an unusual succession arrangement in a country that was formally a hereditary monarchy.

William and Mary accepted the invitation and were crowned on April 11. The form of their coronation oath was new[46]. It addressed the two great constitutional issues of the seventeenth century: the relationship between monarchs and Parliament, and the status of the Protestant Churches and the Church of Rome:

> Will You solemnly Promise and Sweare to Governe the People of this Kingdome of England and the Dominions thereto belonging *according to the Statutes in Parlyament Agreed on and the Laws and Customs of the same* [emphasis added]?
>
> The King and Queene shall say: I solemnly Promise soe to doe . . .
>
> Archbishop or Bishop: Will You to the utmost of Your power *Maintaine the Laws of God the true Profession of the Gospell and the Protestant Reformed Religion Established by Law* [emphasis added]?
>
> King and Queene: All this I Promise to doe . . .

This was a lot more concrete than earlier coronation oaths. There was no reference to the interpretation of laws according to the Laws of God or as agreeable to the Prerogative of Kings. The statutes of Parliament were paramount. The Laws of God were referred to, not as a source of authority but as a body of law to be maintained and were on an equal footing with the Gospel and the Protestant Reformed Religion Established by Law (meaning the Church of England). This oath was a great constitutional innovation.

It is usually said that the last time that England was successfully invaded was in 1066, when William the Conqueror, Duke of Normandy, was victorious at Hastings. Why wasn't the arrival of William with a Dutch-Anglo army in 1688 an invasion?

It is true that William was invited, but that invitation was treasonous. William did not claim the Crown by right of conquest. He accepted it by an invitation from an elected Convention Parliament. That was not a customary form of succession. But James had so completely alienated so many of his subjects, and caused them such alarm and fear, that there was no prospect of the invitation and coronations being successfully challenged at law. Most importantly, in view of: the extent of the rebellions in Britain catalyzed by William's expedition; the fact that half of William's initial military forces were British; and the extent of the financial aid that William had received from many of James' subjects, it is more accurate to see William's military expedition as the most significant event in bringing about the English Revolution than as an invasion.

The form of William and Mary's succession did, however, allow supporters of James (mostly Scottish or Catholic) to maintain the belief that this succession was not lawful. Over the following years there were several rebellions in support of James and his male heirs: an uprising in Ireland led by James in 1689–90; a plot to assassinate William in 1696; a Scottish rebellion in 1698; a Jacobite (meaning a supporter of James II or his male heirs) rising in Scotland and Northumberland, led by James II's son (the "Old Pretender"), in 1715; and the Jacobite rising of 1745 led by "Bonnie Prince Charlie," James II's grandson. Several of these rebellions had French support. The French also planned three invasions, which they expected would be supported by Jacobites in Britain. Two of these plans led to invasion fleets leaving Dunkirk, but neither landed in Britain.

Another great constitutional innovation was the adoption of the Bill of Rights. On January 29, 1689, the Commons had resolved: that "it hath been found; by Experience, to be inconsistent with the Safety and Welfare of this Protestant Kingdom, to be governed by a Popish Prince" and that "a Committee be appointed to bring in general Heads of such things as are absolutely necessary to be considered, for the better securing our Religion, Laws, and Liberties."[47]

The first resolution was a revival of the 1681 proposal to exclude Catholics from the succession to the throne. The second was the genesis of the Bill of Rights. The ultimate result of the resolutions was a statute of December 1689 entitled "An Act declareing the Rights and Liberties of the Subject."[48]

Just as the charge against Charles I contained legal innovations in a practical context, and not in a work of legal or political philosophy, so the Bill of

Rights was grounded in recent events and was not an abstract assertion of ideal rights. It began by listing thirteen ways in which "the late King James the Second" had "endeavour[ed] to subvert and extirpate the Protestant Religion and the Lawes and Liberties of this Kingdome." These included:

- purporting to dispense with and suspend laws without the consent of Parliament;
- purporting to establish an ecclesiastical court;
- imposing taxes without Parliament's approval;
- keeping a standing army without Parliament's approval;
- launching prosecutions in the King's courts which should have been launched in Parliament (which in those days had a judicial function);
- stacking juries;
- imposing excessive fines; and
- inflicting illegal and cruel punishments.

It then enacted legal solutions to these subversive practices. The solutions were a mixture of restrictions on the monarch, and rights of his or her subjects. The restrictions included that the monarch could not:

- dispense with and suspend laws without the consent of Parliament;
- establish ecclesiastical courts;
- tax without Parliament's approval;
- keep a standing army in time of peace without Parliament's approval; and
- stack juries.

The rights of the subjects included:

- for Protestants, to have arms for their defense;
- that there be free elections of members of Parliament;
- immunity for speech in Parliament;
- that bail and fines not be excessive;
- that cruel and unusual punishments not be inflicted; and
- that Parliaments ought to be held frequently.

In 1689 England was, as it is today, a country without a single document as its constitution. Its constitution—the rules and principles by which England is governed—is based on statutes, relevant decisions by authoritative courts, and legal conventions. Authoritative commentaries on the constitution influence how these primary sources are interpreted. In view of the role of precedent (rather than the text of a codified constitution) in this system, innovations are likely to claim to be restatements or amplifications of existing rights or law. And so it was with the Bill of Rights, which was expressed to be "for the Vindicating and Asserting [of the subjects' ancient] Rights and Liberties."

The Bill of Rights did not deal with habeas corpus (the requirement that a person could only be imprisoned or detained pursuant to a lawful charge). Habeas corpus is one of the most fundamental bulwarks against a tyrannical government and had been included in Magna Carta and in the "Habeas Corpus Act" of 1679. Its absence from the 1689 Bill of Rights suggests that there was general compliance with it by that time.

Much of Magna Carta was concerned with rights to and the inheritance of land, and the basic administration of justice. It was a document for a feudal society. The Bill of Rights traversed some of the same ground, but was largely focused on matters relating to Parliament, and the relationship between Parliament and the monarch.

Just what had been achieved since the collapse of James II's regime?

New monarchs had been installed without a major dispute or war in England. James did fight William in Ireland, and there were later Jacobite risings. The threat of Catholics seeking to take power in England was dealt with, and that threat was never credibly repeated. Most fundamentally, it was clearer that the monarch was subject to law; certain individual rights were assured; and the relationship between the monarch and Parliament was partly codified. England had become a constitutional monarchy.

The events of 1688–89 were truly momentous.

The changes introduced in 1688–89 were largely a response to the traumas that had afflicted England as it emerged from the medieval period and broke with the Church of Rome in the mid-sixteenth century, and then had to suffer the Stuarts' ambivalence to the new Church and to Parliament. They were not driven principally by political philosophers. But the changes of 1688–89 did bring intellectual coherence to the English constitution.

The country no longer suffered from the risks and uncertainty inherent in the conflicting residue of medieval beliefs—kings who believed that they were accountable to God alone, and yet were also subject to law; and personal flirtation with the Roman Church, even though staying out of that Church's reach and the reach of the powerful Catholic monarchies was essential to the continued development of England's liberal institutions and values.

The English Revolution achieved astounding constitutional progress. It is often said to have done so with little bloodshed or suffering in England. That is partly because the Revolution is presented as occurring only in 1688–89. This chapter has shown that the events of those years were the culmination of developments that had begun before 1649. The Revolution would not have occurred if the Civil Wars and the trial and beheading of Charles I had not occurred. Charles I's crime was to have committed treason against Parliament and the people, as the alleged supreme source of legal authority in England. Charles II and his brother could not successfully reimpose prerogative rule and Catholicism on a people who, within living memory, had taken that revolutionary action. The violence and bloodshed of the Civil Wars were an integral part of the process that culminated in the Revolutionary coup against James II.

THE ENGLISH REVOLUTION IN NORTH AMERICA

In North America, rumors and then news of the English Revolution led to major rebellions from mid-April 1689 in each of Massachusetts, New York, and Maryland.

The colonies that had been merged into the Dominion of New England (Massachusetts, Connecticut, Rhode Island, New Hampshire, New York, and New Jersey) resumed the separate forms of government that they had enjoyed before the merger or, in the case of Massachusetts, before its charter was revoked.

New York and Maryland also established rebel governments. New York had long been dissatisfied with the legal status of its free colonists' rights to participate in government. As residents of a proprietary and then a Crown colony, they had never enjoyed the clarity of a charter. They had sought one since 1683, partly influenced by Virginians' attempts in 1675 to obtain a charter, rather than being exposed to the risk of arbitrary government through the exercise of the royal prerogative.

Massachusetts achieved a spectacular outcome from the Revolution. In 1691, it was granted a new charter[49]. The new charter did not confer the degree of independence that the blessed 1629 charter had done. The Governor was to be appointed by the monarch. But it did mandate an elected executive council and legislature (the "Generall Court or Assembly") whose members would comprise the Governor, the elected Councilors, and elected representatives. Freedom of Christian worship (except for "Papists") was assured. The colonial government could pass laws which were not repugnant to the laws of England. New laws were subject to a royal veto.

Massachusettans would "have and enjoy all Libertyes and Immunities of Free and naturall Subjects . . . as if they and every of them were borne within this Our Realme of England." This was a repudiation of Charles II's and James II's refusal to accept that colonists had the same legal rights as the English in England. It was a potent principle.

Massachusetts' success was partly a result of the tireless and astute work in London of the colony's principal agent there, Increase Mather. It also reflected that Massachusetts had friends with influence in England, and that William III had come to accept that the history of Massachusetts as a Puritan colony which had enjoyed almost complete independence under its 1629 charter made it appropriate for Massachusetts to have the benefit of a new charter. However, the new charter did give the Crown more power than the 1629 charter had done.

No other colony received a new charter. But all benefitted from the English Revolution which constrained royal power, and increased the political influence of merchants, manufacturers, and the active gentry, at the expense of capricious monarchs and land-owning aristocrats. It had become less likely that the royal prerogative would be used to infringe the core rights of free colonists. In their book *Why Nations Fail: the Origins of Power, Prosperity, and Poverty*, Daron Acemoglu and James A. Robinson describe the Revolution as being of fundamental importance to the emergence of pluralistic political and economic institutions in England, which uniquely enabled that country to breakthrough to sustained economic growth in the eighteenth century[50]. England was increasingly dominated by commercial interests, and the North American colonies had an increasingly important role to play in the commerce of England and its empire.

The arrangements for government in the North American colonies after the English Revolution still contained some of the seeds of the American Revolution, including: the Navigation Act system of trade restrictions and taxes, room for doubt about the extent of the legislative power of the colonial elected assemblies, and differing beliefs in the Colonies and in England as to whether the Americans could be taxed without the consent of their local assemblies.

THE ENGLISH REVOLUTION (CONTINUED)

In England, the political threat posed by Catholics was resolved after the Revolution largely by entrenching discrimination against Catholics. This continued until the "Roman Catholic Relief Act" of 1829.

As well as becoming a constitutional monarchy as a result of the English Revolution, had England become a democracy?

The requirement that the Government must have the confidence of the House of Commons had not yet been developed, so the executive functions of Governments were still conducted by the monarch and his or her Ministers. (By the time of the American Revolution, the norm was that there was a Prime Minister who must have the confidence of the House of Commons, and the Prime Minister chose the other Ministers. Their appointment was formalized by the monarch. See chapter 4.)

Under Charles II the voting franchise had reverted to the franchise before the English Civil Wars. This remained the case in 1689, except that Catholics had lost the vote. The voting franchise was not substantially broadened until the great Reform Act of 1832.

The influence of the monarch in government and the limited voting franchise meant that England could not in 1689 be said to be a democratic constitutional monarchy.

While discrimination against Catholics solved a political problem, it was not very Christian. John Locke,[51] the great philosopher, wrote "A Letter Concerning Toleration," first published in 1689.[52] Locke's arguments included that:

- Christianity recognizes the separation of earthly power and religious conviction, and the religious beliefs of an individual are not a matter over which the State should assert authority; and
- as Christian faith is based in belief (or the "inward persuasion of the mind"), it cannot be compelled.

The first of these arguments is, and was when Locke wrote, well enough understood. Christianity does not teach that the State should be controlled by the Church—it is not "theocratic."

The second proposition strikes us as obvious. That is because in the modern world many people have the prosperity and opportunity to exercise some choice in their lives, and opinion or belief often precedes choice. Modern culture is highly self-conscious. Medieval culture was not. Locke was writing when the belief that people are self-conscious creatures capable of individual choice was not widespread.

Locke was unusually well placed to make the argument in 1689, because his philosophical enquiries had extended to the nature of the self, and the central role of the conscious mind in the individual's understanding of the world. His belief contrasts with the pre-Renaissance perception of the person, which was not so much of self-conscious individuals but more of people who had functions and who did things according to custom and their position or role in the economy and in the social system.

It is much easier to believe that religious belief can be adopted or compelled if religious belief is seen as a matter of custom and convention than if it is seen as a matter of the "inward persuasion of the mind."

Religion played so large a role in people's lives at the time of the English Revolution, and the Roman Catholic Church was so rich and powerful, that

territorial and dynastic ambitions could easily be coupled with sectarian religious issues.

Locke was right—it was wrong to discriminate against Catholics. But after
the suffering caused by Bloody Mary and the uncertainty and risk caused by
the Stuarts' flirtation with and conversion to Catholicism, keeping Catholics
out of positions of power was a pragmatic restriction.

As noted at the beginning of this chapter, the English Rump Parliament had
charged Charles I with "a wicked design to erect and uphold in himself an unlimited and tyrannical power to rule according to his Will, and to overthrow
the Rights and Liberties of the People." The constitutional changes introduced during the English Revolution established Parliamentary supremacy[53]
in England and made it unlawful for any future English monarch to exercise
tyrannical power.

But as was also noted at the beginning of this chapter, some 90 years after
the English Revolution, the American Declaration of Independence of 1776
charged George III with a history of actions "all having in direct Object the
Establishment of an absolute Tyranny over these [American] States." The
Declaration was referring to actions of George III and Parliament which specifically conflicted with or infringed the rights which colonists in America
believed that they had under English law. George III did not disregard or
suppress Parliament, as Charles I and his sons had done. The Declaration was
charging George III with tyranny in the American colonies, not in the British
Isles. There is no contradiction between the kings and queens of Britain having ceased to be tyrants at home but trammelling fundamental political rights
which British-Americans believed that they had in the colonies.

NOTES

1. "An Act of the Commons of England Assembled in Parliament, for Erecting of a
High Court of Justice, for the Trying and Judging of Charles Stuart, King of England.
January 1649." *Acts and Ordinances of the Interregnum, 1642–1660*, ed. C H Firth
and R S R S Rait (London, 1911), pp. 1253–1255. British History Online. Accessed
July 2018 to July 2020. http://www.british-history.ac.uk/no-series/acts-ordinances
-interregnum/pp1253-1255.

2. Stuart, James (King James VI of Scotland and James I of England). *The Trve
Lawe of free Monarchies: Or, The Reciprock and Mvtvall Dvtie Betwixt a free King,
and his naturall Subjectes.* London, 1616: British Library. Accessed July 2018.
https://www.bl.uk/collection-items/the-true-law-of-free-monarchies-by-king-james
-vi-and-i.

3. Foxe, John. 1563. *Foxe's Book Of Martyrs.* Knight and Son, 1856. Open Library. Accessed August 2018. https://openlibrary.org/books/OL1586721M/Foxe's _book_of_martyrs.

4. At the time, there were 224 German speaking states, mostly principalities. They were not consolidated into Germany and Austria until 1871.

5. "Entire ceremonies of the coronations of His Majesty King Charles II. and of her Majesty Queen Mary, Consort to James II: As published by those learned heralds Ashmole and Sandford" 1761. Printed for Owen and others. Eighteenth Century Collections Online, University of Michigan, Text Creation Partnership. Accessed August to December 2018. https://quod.lib.umich.edu/e/ecco/004895348.0001.000/1:6.1?rgn =div2;view=toc.

6. "Magna Carta, 1215." London: British Museum, 1963, translated by Davis, G. R. C., pp. 23–33, published online by the British Library. Accessed July 2018. https:// www.bl.uk/magna-carta/articles/magna-carta-english-translation#.

7. "Magna Carta, 1297." (25_Edw_1_cc_1_9_29) legislation.gov.uk. Accessed July to September 2018. https://www.legislation.gov.uk/aep/Edw1cc1929/25/9 /introduction.

8. ("Magna Carta, 1297" 25_Edw_1_cc_1_9_29).

9. Habeas corpus began as a prerogative of the king, to ascertain whether his subjects were being unlawfully detained by a local nobleman, but it morphed into also being a protection of the subject against any unlawful imprisonment.

10. Shakespeare's *King John*, written during the reign of Elizabeth I, did not mention Magna Carta even though the granting of the Great Charter was the most significant event of John's reign. Elizabeth would not have welcomed her subjects being reminded of a successful rebellion against the Crown, and that a King had been forced to accept specific limits on his power.

11. Bragg, Melvyn. 2012. *The Book of Books.* Hodder & Stoughton, describes the history and significance of this version of the Bible.

12. There is a parallel with the disintermediation of information and the publication of misinformation in the early age of the internet.

13. At 4,470,000 it was almost back to its level of 1347. In 1348 the Black Death arrived and killed some 45 percent of the population.

14. On British economic growth, Broadberry, Stephen; Guan, Hanhui; and Li, David Daokui. "China, Europe And The Great Divergence: A Study In Historical National Accounting, 980–1850" (University of Oxford, *Discussion Papers in Economics and Social History*, Number 155 April 2017). Accessed October 2018. https:// www.economics.ox.ac.uk/materials/working_papers/2839/155aprilbroadberry.pdf.

15. Friel, Ian. 2009. "Elizabethan Merchant Ships and Shipbuilding" Gresham College, lecture at the Museum of London. Accessed August 2018. https://www .gresham.ac.uk/lectures-and-events/elizabethan-merchant-ships-and-shipbuilding.

16. "Petition of Right," 1628. The National Archives (U.K.). Accessed June to September 2018. http://www.nationalarchives.gov.uk/pathways/citizenship/rise_par liament/transcripts/petition_right.htm.

17. Gardiner, S. R. (editor). 1906. "Protestation Of The House Of Commons. March 2, 1629," in *The Constitutional Documents of the Puritan Revolution,*

1625–1660. Clarendon Press, 1906, page 104. The Online Library Of Liberty. Accessed June to September 2018. http://oll-resources.s3.amazonaws.com/titles/1434/Gardiner_046.

18. "Republic" is from the Latin "res" meaning affair, matter, or thing and "publicus" meaning of the people, or public.

19. Who could vote in elections for the English House of Commons at this time? In the counties or countryside, men (by custom rather than a specific gender requirement) who were freeholders of property worth at least forty shillings. In the boroughs or towns, the right to vote was usually dependent on residence, a property qualification or status as a freeman, or some mixture of these. In some boroughs the franchise was restricted to members of the corporation running the borough. Each of Oxford and Cambridge Universities was represented by men elected by members of the Senate of the University.

20. When the impeachment case failed against the Earl of Strafford in 1641, the Commons executed him anyway, using the political process of a bill of attainder. Bills of attainder are prohibited by the American Constitution.

21. The death toll of the wars in England, Scotland, and Ireland between 1639 and 1660 was horrific. Estimates vary widely and may not be reliable. They were almost certainly the most devastating wars in British history. Including deaths in battle, and from consequent disease and famine, estimates vary from some 4 percent in England to 20 percent in Ireland.

22. Fritze, Ronald H., Robison, William B. 1996. *Historical Dictionary of Stuart England, 1603–1689*. William, Greenwood Press. Page 118.

23. For a translation of Act of Abjuration of 1581 (Dutch). *The Library of Original Sources* ed Thatcher, Oliver J. University Research Extension Co., c1907, Volume 5, page 190. Internet Archive. Accessed June 2018, July 2020. https://archive.org/details/libraryoforigina05thatuoft/page/190/mode/2up.

24. ("Act of the Commons of England Assembled in Parliament, for Erecting of a High Court of Justice, for the Trying and Judging of Charles Stuart, King of England. January 1649")

25. After the restoration of the monarchy, a piece of legislation was passed known as the "Indemnity and Oblivion Act" of 1660 ("Charles II, 1660: An Act of Free and Generall Pardon Indempnity [sic] and Oblivion." *Statutes of the Realm*: Volume 5, 1628–80, ed. John Raithby (s.l, 1819), pp. 226–234. British History Online. Accessed July 2018 to September 2018. http://www.british-history.ac.uk/statutes-realm/vol5/pp226-234). It "put in utter oblivion" acts of the Commonwealth and the Protectorate (the two forms of government in the republican period) which had purported to be legally valid.

26. The sentence usually faced by a commoner who was found guilty of high treason was grizzly—a man would be hanged, but not to break his neck or to kill him. Then his genitals were cut off, his abdomen cut and some of his guts pulled out and burnt while he watched. He was then decapitated, and his body was cut in four. The punishment for a woman was less brutal. Aristocrats or prominent people were merely beheaded.

27. This description draws on several sources, but, in particular, Robertson, Geoffrey. 2005. *The Tyrannicide Brief*. Chatto & Windus. That book is a forceful response to the customary dismissal of the trial and execution as the murdering of the King without any legal basis. Robertson also argues convincingly that the trial of Charles I for tyranny was the precursor to modern trials for crimes against humanity and war crimes.

28. "Articles of Impeachment of King Charles I, 1649." *The Trial of Charles I*, edited by Lockyer, Roger; London: The Folio Society; 1959; pp. 82–85. Accessed July 2018 to July 2020. https://en.wikisource.org/wiki/Articles_of_Impeachment_of _King_Charles_I.

29. This book does not deal with the period in which England is or was subject to the laws of the European Union. In that Union, legislation cannot be initiated by the European Parliament.

30. In *1688: The First Modern Revolution*. Yale University Press, 2009, Professor Pincus convincingly makes the case for this Revolution as the first momentous modern European revolution.

31. "The Instrument of Government." American Historical Documents. Original Sources. Accessed August 2018. www.originalsources.com/Document.aspx ?DocID=Y9YT23252Q2UKKY. Other than from 1653 to the end of the Protectorate, England has not had a codified constitution. Its system of government has been based on statute, relevant decisions by authoritative Courts, and legal conventions.

32. Rhode Island had received a patent from a Parliamentary Committee in 1644.

33. Lovejoy, David S. 1972. *The Glorious Revolution in America*. Harper & Row is an invaluable guide to the differences between the colonists on the one hand and the Crown and proprietors on the other in the decades preceding the English or Glorious Revolution in 1688–89, and on other aspects of the constitutional history of the North American colonies in this period.

34. William was the hereditary Prince of the Principality of Orange, now in Provence, France. He was also the Stadtholder of five provinces in the Dutch Republic (the highest office in those provinces). That position was not yet hereditary. William's mother was Mary, daughter of Charles I of England.

35. Unless the American War of Independence is classified as an English civil war, as it is sometimes.

36. (Pincus 2009), especially chapters 5 and 6. Pincus emphasizes the large extent of the changes that James was making to the English state, and not just his Catholicizing, as a cause of the English Revolution.

37. The use of the Crown's reserve power to prorogue Parliament became contentious in 2019, when Prime Minister Boris Johnson sought to prorogue Parliament for five weeks, in the lead up to a Brexit deadline. On September 24, 2019, the British Supreme Court ruled that the Prime Minister's attempt to 'prorogue' Parliament was invalid. The power to prorogue is a surviving ancient Crown power (a "prerogative power"). By 2019, the power was exercised by the monarch on the advice of the Prime Minister, and the monarch always followed the Prime Minister's advice. The British Supreme Court held that Prime Minister Johnson's advice to the Queen—that Parliament should be prorogued—was legally invalid, because prorogation would

have had the effect, without reasonable justification, of frustrating Parliament's ability to carry out its constitutional functions. A copy of the judgment ([2019] UKSC 41) is at: https://www.supremecourt.uk/cases/docs/uksc-2019-0192-judgment .pdf

38. Copies of "Two Papers written by the Late King Charles II together with a Copy of a Paper written by the late Duchess of York." Volume 2: February 5, 1685–December 8, 1688, in *Calendar of Treasury Papers*, Volume 1, 1556–1696, ed. Joseph Redington (London, 1868), pp. 15–31. British History Online. Accessed August 2018. http://www.british-history.ac.uk/cal-treasury-papers/vol1/pp15-31.

39. "Declaration of Indulgence of King James II, April 4, 1687." The Jacobite Heritage. Accessed August 2018. https://web.archive.org/web/20040227140532 /http://www.jacobite.ca/documents/16870404.htm.

40. "Letter of invitation to William of Orange, 1688." The Jacobite Heritage. Accessed August 2018. http://jacobite.ca/documents/16880630.htm.

41. "Prince of Orange's declaration: 19 December 1688." *Journal of the House of Commons*: Volume 10, 1688–1693 (London, 1802), pp. 1–6. British History Online. Accessed June to August 2018. http://www.british-history.ac.uk/commons -jrnl/vol10/pp1-6.

42. "Letter from General Churchill to James II, 23 November 1688." The Jacobite Heritage. Accessed July to September 2018. http://www.jacobite.ca /documents/1688churchill.htm.

43. "House of Commons Journal Volume 10: 22 January 1689," in *Journal of the House of Commons*: Volume 10, 1688–1693 (London, 1802), pp. 9–12. British History Online. Accessed July 2018. http://www.british-history.ac.uk/commons-jrnl/vol 10/pp9-12.

44. ("House of Commons Journal Volume 10: 22 January 1689")

45. "House of Commons Journal Volume 10: 28 January 1689," in *Journal of the House of Commons*: Volume 10, 1688–1693 (London, 1802), p. 14. British History Online. Accessed August 2018 to July 2020. http://www.british-history.ac.uk /commons-jrnl/vol10/p14

46. "William and Mary, 1688: An Act for Establishing the Coronation Oath." [Chapter VI. Rot. Parl. pt. 5. nu. 3.], in *Statutes of the Realm*: Volume 6, 1685–94, ed. John Raithby (s.l, 1819), pp. 56–57. British History Online. Accessed August 2018. https://www.british-history.ac.uk/statutes-realm/vol6/pp56-57.

47. "English Bill of Rights, 1689," 1 William & Mary Sess 2 c 2. The Avalon Project, Yale Law School. Accessed july 2018 to July 2020. https://avalon.law.yale .edu/17th_century/england.asp.

48. "William and Mary, 1688: An Act declareing the Rights and Liberties of the Subject and Setleing the Succession of the Crowne" [Chapter II. Rot. Parl. pt. 3. nu. 1.], in *Statutes of the Realm*: Volume 6, 1685–89, ed. John Raithby (s.l, 1819). Accessed August 17, 2018. British History Online: http://www.british-history.ac.uk /statutes-realm/vol6/pp142-145.

49. ("Charter of Massachusetts Bay, 1691")

50. Acemoglu, Daron and Robinson, James A. 2012. *Why Nations Fail: the Origins of Power, Prosperity, and Poverty*. Crown Business, pp. 102-104 and chapter 7.

51. Locke had a strong American connection. He was the principal author of the first proposed colonial constitution of Carolina (named for Charles I, and now North Carolina, South Carolina, and Georgia).

52. Locke, John. 1689. "A Letter Concerning Toleration." Accessed August 2018. Internet Archive: https://archive.org/details/toleration/mode/2up.

53. This supremacy is not absolute. Parliament's power to make laws may be qualified by, for example, treaties or the devolution of powers to legislatures in Scotland, Wales, and Northern Ireland. But the phrase "Parliamentary supremacy" is a useful summation in some contexts, where the key point is that Parliament is now more potent in England than the Crown and the Government.

Chapter Three

The Original Legislature

The Origins of Parliament

This chapter briefly tells how the British Parliament of the American Revolutionary period came about. The importance of the development of Parliament for the American Constitution was profound. As we have seen, in the seventeenth century Parliament had insisted that the king was subject to law, and that he could not circumvent its control of revenue and the law-making process.

Parliament had been regarded by American colonists as the great bulwark and security of their liberties and privileges. Parliament's failure to directly represent the colonists and its failure to control the king and his Ministers were two of the Founders' most significant criticisms of the British Government in the period leading up to the Declaration.

When Americans came to draft the State constitutions of the Revolutionary period, they placed elected representative assemblies at the center of their systems of government. Those assemblies were adaptations of the American colonial assemblies. But Parliament was the preeminent assembly in the British colonial system of government. Many of the Framers were familiar with the functions and workings of Parliament.

Government is often conceived as having three main functions: a law-making or legislative function; an executive function of doing things (or executing), including the policing of law and regulatory enforcement, implementing government policies, representing and defending the nation, and administering the activities of the State;[1] and a judicial function of determining the application of law in individual cases, including both civil disputes and criminal law-enforcement.

By the American Revolutionary period, the British Parliament not only controlled revenue, and originated and passed legislation; it also provided and oversaw the members of the executive government (the Prime Minister and other Ministers—see chapter 4). Parliament also had a limited judicial function (it lost this function in 2009).

When and how did Parliament originate? Its roots have not been traced to any form of assembly of the Britons, the people who had populated the region that the Romans called "Britannia." Some historians have traced the origins of the English Parliament to the folkmoot (meaning "meeting of the people"), a form of assembly said to have been brought to England by the Angles, Saxons, and Jutes, who invaded and occupied part of Britain over some two hundred years from around 400 CE[2] (when the Romans left).

The Angles, Saxons, and Jutes were "English," a term derived from "Angles." Old English is a Germanic language derived from the dialects of the invaders. "England" has the same derivation, and roughly corresponds to the area which the new arrivals came to dominate. The Britons either stayed in England and adopted the culture and language of the smaller Anglo-Saxon[3] population or fled to Brittany (in modern France), Galicia (in modern Spain), Cornwall, Wales, or southern Scotland. If the Britons did have assemblies, they were displaced by the folkmoots of the new rulers.

England became a single kingdom under Athelstan, who reigned 927–939 CE. Local folkmoots survived unification. The national assembly of England was a witenagemot, an assembly of the wise. It comprised bishops, ealdormen (as representatives of the shires), and King's thanes (who were landholders under a duty to fight for the King). The powers of this national assembly were potentially large, but variable. It could elect kings and depose them. It was involved with the king in making rules or legislation and in nominating ealdormen and bishops. Its approval was needed before taxes were imposed. However, the scope of national government was small at that time, and if the king was competent the witenagemot was not assertive.

Whether advisory assemblies to the English kings owed their origins to a type of assembly that the Anglo-Saxon invaders brought with them from their homelands in the north of modern Germany and the Jutland peninsula in modern Denmark or were substantially of a form that developed after their arrival in England, is not important for our purposes. What matters is:

- that there were advisory or representative assemblies from at least Anglo-Saxon times;
- that a single national assembly developed;
- how members of the national assembly were appointed or elected, and how that changed;
- who sat in that assembly, and how that changed;
- that Parliament developed two chambers, which became the House of Lords and the House of Commons; and
- that the elected Commons became the more powerful chamber.

After William, Duke of Normandy, conquered England and became king in 1066 (generally referred to as "the Conquest") he held Court three times a year, when he was in England and not in Normandy: "Thrice he bare his crown each year, as oft as he was in England. . . . And then were with him all the rich men over all England: archbishops and diocesan bishops, abbots, earls, thanes, and knights. *So very stern was he also and hot, that no man durst do anything against his will* [emphasis added] . . ."[4]

This description emphasized that the King's most powerful subjects were at Court not to assert their own rights or powers, but so that the King could impose his will on them. Through the men assembled at Court, the King controlled his Kingdom.

A smaller group than "all the rich men over all England," taken from the clergy and barons, conducted the administration of the Kingdom. When it dealt with financial business, this group was known as the Exchequer, named after the checked tablecloth used at its meetings, which was convenient for counting money. The smaller group also formed an executive council, and the King's law court. This group, which we would call the King's "ministers," operated with looser oversight from the King when he was in Normandy.

Clause 14 of the Magna Carta of 1215 set out the principle that taxes could not be imposed without the consent of an assembly:

> To obtain the general consent of the realm for the assessment of [taxes], we will cause the archbishops, bishops, abbots, earls, and greater barons to be summoned individually. . . . To those who hold lands directly of us we will cause a general summons to be issued, through the sheriffs and other officials. . . . When a summons has been issued, the business appointed for the day shall go forward in accordance with the resolution of those present, even if not all those who were summoned have appeared.

There are several important things about this clause, remembering that it is contained in a Charter which rebel feudal lords or barons had imposed on King John (a great-great grandson of William the Conqueror), and which was not always complied with. The first is that it provided that taxes could not be imposed without the consent of the assembly.

The second is that the assembly included not only the leading churchmen and greater barons (who were summoned individually), but also any person who held lands directly from the King. William the Conqueror had granted land (subject to the landholder meeting feudal obligations) to many of his followers and supporters, mostly Normans. There were about 170 of them after the Conquest, including the greater barons. The lesser barons were summoned by a general summons, not an individual summons. This distinction may look like an early form of the distinction between the Lords and the

Commons. But the lesser barons were summoned in their personal capacities as landowners who had been granted land by the King, not as representatives of their counties or shires. And the towns were not represented under the clause 14 procedure. So clause 14 described a purely feudal body of the leading churchmen and people who held land from the King and who were subject to feudal obligations to him.

The third thing about the quoted clause is that it contained administrative detail about how the assembly was to be convened, and stated that the assembly would conduct business of which notice had been given. Clause 14 was not a waffly statement of aspiration. It was the barons' intention that this assembly would be a real functioning body, dealing with real business.

Between 1215 and 1295, several national assemblies were summoned. The first known use of the word "Parlement" to describe the assembly of notables was in 1236 ("parler" is the French verb meaning "to speak").

For the assembly of 1254, sheriffs of counties were instructed to send Knights of the Shire to parliament to advise the King on finance. What was important about this was that the people summoned did not include the lesser barons. The summons was for representatives of the counties who had to be chosen by the landowners of the county for this purpose. This was significant—the assembly had become in part representative and elected. It was no longer simply feudal.

The Parliament of 1265 went further. For it, two knights from each shire and, for the first time, representatives of the major towns, were summoned. This was an unusual Parliament, though. It was convened while Simon de Montfort, and not the King, was in effect running the government. Summonses were issued to people who were likely to support de Montford's Government. Most barons did not receive a summons.

In 1295, a Parliament was summoned by the King which provides the model for later Parliaments. Archbishops, bishops, and senior clergy were summoned. Seven earls and forty-one barons were summoned by name. The sheriff of each shire was directed to cause two knights of the shire, two citizens of each city, and two burgesses of each borough to be elected, and to attend[5]. (A "borough" is a town with some degree of self-government.) There was no general system for how elections were to be conducted, and the methods varied widely in the shires, cities, and boroughs.

The Archbishops, bishops and senior clergy were summoned "*to consider, ordain and provide* [emphasis added], along with us [the King] and with the rest of the prelates and principal men and other inhabitants of our kingdom" how the business of the Parliament should be dealt with.

"To consider" implies a role in the decision-making process, but not to make decisions. The prelates participated in the making of decisions, but as advisors. The King was the decision-maker.

The prelates' role was also "to ordain." The Latin root of "to ordain" is "ordinare," meaning to put in order, arrange, dispose, or appoint. The role of the prelates was also to acknowledge and support the decisions of Parliament.

Their role was also "to provide." The Church would be expected to provide money to help implement the decisions of the Parliament. The Church at this time had vast landholdings, and other sources of revenue.

The earls and barons were summoned *"for considering, ordaining and doing* [emphasis added] along with us [the King] and with the prelates, and the rest of the principal men and other inhabitants of our kingdom . . ."* Doing* would include both contributing funds and getting the job done—including, potentially, military service.

The representative members' role did not include to consider or ordain:

> . . . we strictly require you to cause two knights from the aforesaid county, two citizens from each city in the same county, and two burgesses from each borough . . . to come to us. . . . Moreover, the said knights are to have full and sufficient power for themselves and for the community of the aforesaid county, and the said citizens and burgesses for themselves and the communities of the aforesaid cities and boroughs separately . . . *for doing what shall then be ordained according to the common counsel* [emphasis added].

The representative members were to have power to bind their communities to the decisions made by the King after consultation with the prelates, earls, and barons. The representative members were not summoned to participate in the making of the decisions. Even the verbs with which they were summoned were different from the principal men, who were "commanded" to attend: the sheriff was "required to cause" the representative members to attend. Their role was to be on time, to pay taxes, and to implement decisions.

In summary, the King led the executive branch of government (the administrative and "doing" branch), advised and supported by a small group of ministers. On major questions of policy, legislation, and revenue, he consulted with the great Lords and leaders of the Church. He involved representatives of his property-owning subjects in the decision-making process and bound them to his decisions. The Church, Lords and property-owning subjects provided funds. The Lords and the representative members supported the King and his ministers in implementing decisions.

In 1295, not all proposed statutes were submitted to Parliament. Some statutes were made by the King with a great council of Church leaders and the barons, without any lesser clergy, lesser landowners or townspeople being represented. This is hardly surprising. The existence of such a great council, which is more feudal in form than Parliament, is consistent with an incomplete evolution from a government organised on feudal principles towards institutions of government which represented people with substantial or moderate property—from a kingdom organised for military service by landholders, to a kingdom organised for supplying the Crown with the revenue to hire military forces when necessary. The role of the great council declined over time, and Parliament came to displace it.

During the fourteenth century, the representative members began to sit separately from the Lords and prelates. The House of Commons[6] and the House of Lords came into being. Initially the House of Lords was the more important chamber. The Commons' separation from the Lords however meant that the Commons began to deal with real business and make decisions, and not merely to do what the King and Lords had ordained.

During the reign of Edward III in 1340, a statute was passed which provided that no direct taxes would be imposed without Parliament's consent—an updated and more authoritative statement of the principle in clause 14 of the original Magna Carta. Later in the 1300s, the Commons (which represented the people who would have to pay most of any tax) acquired the prime role in approving a new tax, with the Lords assenting.

There are two astonishing things about a statute of 1429, in the reign of Henry VI, which dealt with the voting franchise in the shires.[7] The first is that it restricted rather than expanded the category of people who could vote in elections. The history of representation in Parliament is not a smooth progression from the representation of chiefs or nobles only, towards the representation of all adults. The second is that this restricted franchise lasted for a staggering 400 years—until the Reform Act of 1832.

The pretext for the restricted franchise was that the former franchise was a threat to law and order:

> . . . whereas in many counties the elections of knights of the shires, those chosen to attend the king's parliaments, have of late been carried out by too great and excessive a number of people dwelling within those same counties, *of whom the larger part have been people of little substance or of no worth . . . whereby homicides, riots, assaults, and feuds are very likely to arise* . . . unless a suitable remedy is provided . . . [emphasis added].

No law-and-order problem had yet arisen. Landowners were using their influence with the King and in Parliament to limit the franchise in their own interests, in alleged anticipation of a possible law and order problem.

The new franchise was: "persons dwelling and resident therein, each of whom shall have a freehold to the value of at least forty shillings a year."

Note that the test not only favoured property, but a particular type of property: freehold land. Over time with inflation of asset values, more people met the requirement of having a freehold of at least forty shillings a year, so the franchise incrementally widened.

There was no national law dealing with how the boroughs' representatives were to be chosen, and the proportion of the population in the boroughs who participated in elections varied widely: "In the . . . boroughs the qualification [varied] between a wide democracy and the narrowest oligarchy."[8]

Some boroughs became known as "rotten boroughs," the most infamous example of which was Old Sarum. The former town of that name had become a hamlet in the thirteenth century and had ceased to exist by the fourteenth century. Nonetheless, it retained its right to send two representatives to Parliament until 1832. The right was exercised by the landowners of the site of the former town. Rotten boroughs obviously gave landowners disproportionate influence in the Commons. They already had it in the Lords since nobles generally had country estates.

From 1535, Wales was represented in the Commons—one of several changes which saw Wales fully incorporated into the English administrative and legal system.

In the sixteenth century, after Henry VIII established the Church of England and suppressed the monasteries, the only prelates in the House of Lords (the "Lords Spiritual") were archbishops and bishops. The earls and barons who were personally summoned to sit in Parliament had been succeeded by nobles of five ranks: dukes, marquesses, earls, viscounts, and barons. Those titles had become hereditary. For the first time there were more nobles in the House of Lords (the "Lords Temporal") than Lords Spiritual.

The monarch had significant influence over the composition of the House of Lords. He or she in effect appointed the archbishops and bishops, the Lords Spiritual. The monarch could also create new Lords Temporal, or peers. The Tudor monarchs did not create many new peerages. But James I did, nearly doubling their number. Charles II created many more, rewarding his supporters in the Restoration. One hundred and forty-five peers, and twenty-six Lords Spiritual, were summoned to the Parliament of 1685.

As for the size of the House of Commons: by 1677 it had 513 members—twenty-four for Wales, eighty for the English counties, four for Oxford and Cambridge Universities, and 405 for the English boroughs. There was no change in the number of English or Welsh representatives until 1832. Forty-five Scottish members were added when Scotland joined the union of England and Wales in 1707. There were no American members. One hundred Irish members were added on the union of Ireland with England, Wales, and Scotland in 1801.

The following paragraphs include data and developments that relate to economic, demographic, and political changes that were in progress at the time of the American Revolutionary period, even though some of the events occurred after that period. They help to provide context relevant to the Revolutionary period, including that in that period Parlement was not adequately representative of that part of the British population in the British Isles that had economic power and political aspirations. This may have contributed to it being less attuned to the position of British Americans than it would have been if, for example, trade and manufacturing interests were better represented in the Commons.

Between 1700 and 1820, the population of England increased from 5.2 million to 10.4 million. In 1700, 56 percent of the workforce had been employed in agriculture, 22 percent in industry and 22 percent in services. In 1820, the proportions were 37 percent, 33 percent, and 30 percent, respectively. In 1700, 13.3 percent of the population lived in towns or cities with more than 10,000 people. In 1800, the proportion was 20.3 percent of the much larger population.

GDP per capita in England increased in the same period by 50 percent—since 1500 it had roughly doubled. Of course, a 50 percent increase per capita when the population has doubled is a tripling of aggregate GDP, which means that England had become much more prosperous and potent during this period. These growth rates are not high by the standards of prosperous countries in the last 200 years, but they were unprecedented by historical standards and were accelerating quickly in the early nineteenth century.[9]

Importantly, as the economy grew, and new products and technologies were applied, the range of economic activity and supply chains became more complex. There were more businesses, all of which had owners. Work became more complicated and specialised. More people became skilled and economically empowered.[10]

These changes did not look good for an aristocracy based in the countryside and trying to maintain its hugely disproportionate influence in Parliament. The rising industrial and middle class that these data imply were likely to consider that the allocation of political power needed to change.

The Representation of the People Act 1832 (generally called the Reform Act of 1832) was momentous. It dramatically enlarged the voting franchise. It redrew electoral boundaries and enfranchised industrial towns and cities.

As for the House of Lords, after the Restoration the House of Commons had asserted that proposed legislation for raising revenue could not be amended by the House of Lords. In 1701, the Commons proposed legislation, which was in part for raising revenue, and in part for another purpose. The

Commons asserted that the Lords could not amend it. The Lords submitted, rather than allow the supply of revenue to be delayed.

As the adage has it: "Who pays the piper calls the tune." Once the Commons could control the approval of revenue for the Government, the Commons was clearly the more powerful of the two Houses.

NOTES

1. The "State" is, in this context, the nation as a legal entity. The "Government" is, in this context, the group of Ministers which oversees the activities of the State (as well as determining the policies that they wish to apply in that process). In every-day speech, "Government" is often used to mean the State, or the Government and the State.

2. CE means "Common Era" a secularized version of AD meaning after the "anno Domini": the year of the birth of Jesus Christ.

3. "Anglo-Saxon" is the umbrella term for the Germanic invaders of England. Not all of them were Angles or Saxons, and many Angles and Saxons did not join the invasion. The term was originally used to distinguish the Germanic population of England from Germanic populations in continental Europe.

4. *The Anglo-Saxon Chronicle*. Translation by Rev. James Ingram 1823. Everyman Press,1912, London, p142. Accessed August 2018. Internet Archive: https://archive.org/stream/Anglo-saxonChronicles/anglo_saxon_chronicle_djvu.txt.

5. For the summonses to the 1295 Parliament: *Translations and Reprints from the Original Sources of European history*. 1897. Translated by E. P. Cheyney. University of Pennsylvania Press. Accessed August 2018. Fordham University: https://sourcebooks.fordham.edu/source/ed1-summons.asp

6. The original meaning of "Commons" was "representatives of communities or corporations."

7. For an extract of the text of the statute 8 Henry VI: "On Elections to Parliament (1429)." Constitution Society. Accessed September 2018. http://constitution.org/sech/sech_069.htm.

8. Maitland, F. W. 1908. Lectures given in 1888. *The Constitutional History of England*. Cambridge University Press, p. 175. Maitland's is a magisterial book, which has been a valuable source for this chapter and for chapter 4.

9. The principal source for these data is Broadberry, S., Campbell, B., Klein, A., Overton, M., & Van Leeuwen, B. 2015. *British Economic Growth, 1270–1870*. Cambridge University Press. doi:10.1017/CBO9781107770760.

10. Of course, many other people remained in desperate poverty.

Chapter Four

The British Executive

The Prime Minister Supersedes the King

The seventeenth century was full of violence and drama for the English constitution. It began with the death of Elizabeth I, an astute monarch who had led England on its path to immense prosperity and influence. It included the trial and execution of Charles I, a king who believed that he was above the law and could not accept that he had to share power with some of his subjects. As we saw in chapter 2, near the century's end Charles' son James II was deposed after pursuing bizarrely ahistorical policies.

By the end of the seventeenth century, the allocation of power between the monarch and Parliament was finally settled in the English Revolution. The monarch still governed but accepted that he or she really was subject to law, and that Parliament had a central role in making laws and keeping a check on government.

The eighteenth century too saw change in the English constitution. But the change happened without civil war or the arrival of a Dutch prince. It happened gradually and almost invisibly—more an evolution than a revolution. The evolution occurred in the way the executive function of government worked. The outcome was that, in substance, England became a disguised republic.

As noted in chapter 3, the executive function is the function of doing things or getting the job done ("executing"). This includes the policing of law and regulatory enforcement, implementing government policies, representing and defending the nation, and administering the activities of the state. The executive function is not the function of making laws or the function of doing justice. It is the function which today in Britain is led by the Prime Minister and his or her Ministers—today collectively referred to as "the Government." At its core is the Prime Minister and a group of the most important Ministers, "the Cabinet."

There are confused descriptions about how the executive branch operates today in the Westminster system of government.[1] It is sometimes said that in this system there is a separation of powers between different branches of government.

The "separation of powers" is a theory of the structure of government under which no person should be involved in more than one functional branch of government: usually described as the legislative, the executive and the judicial branches. Tyranny or an oppressive government is less likely if power is not too concentrated. The Framers of the American Constitution strongly believed in the need for a separation of powers because they were determined that their scheme would not enable tyranny. The English constitution developed a less doctrinaire alternative.

Parliament obviously has a legislative function—a function of proposing and making laws. Bills are introduced to Parliament, submitted three times to each House, debated, often amended and, if passed on a vote, sent to the monarch for his or her assent. But Parliament also has several roles in the executive function. The Prime Minister is chosen from and by the House of Commons, his or her Ministers are chosen by the Prime Minister from members of Parliament, the Government will fall if it loses the confidence of Parliament, and the Government is dependent on Parliament approving the supply of money to it. The extensive overlap between the legislative and executive functions means that the structure of British government has only a partial separation of powers.

The executive branch evolved in Britain by practice and convention, not by legislation or amendment of a written constitution (Britain does not have one). From the time of the English Revolution there were three phases in the development of the executive:

- the first, from the English Revolution until the reign of George I (which began in 1714), in which the "Cabinet Council" developed. That Council was a small group of key advisers to the monarch, with the monarch remaining the final decision-maker in executive government;
- the second, from 1714 until the time of the great Parliamentary and other reforms of the 1830s, in which this Cabinet system continued, but with a member of the Cabinet (the "Prime Minister") rather than the monarch coming to play the leading role, and with Parliament still passing many specific statutes dealing with executive matters; and
- the third, from the reforms of the 1830s, in which the cabinet system under the leadership of the Prime Minister continued, with Parliament being less active in passing executive statutes. The third phase occurred after the American Constitution was ratified—so it is dealt with only briefly in this book.

After William and Mary accepted the throne in 1689, William personally led the executive, as monarchs had done since ancient times. William's experience of governing had not been as an absolute monarch—he was the Stadtholder (the most senior executive officer) of five of the seven provinces of the Dutch Republic and was accustomed to working in a republican system of government.

In England under William and Mary, an inner circle of councilors emerged. That circle became known as the "Cabinet Council" ("cabinet" being a now archaic word for a small private room, of the type in which this inner council is likely to have met). The influence of the wider Privy Council declined as the power of the Cabinet Council increased.

By the reign of Mary's sister Anne, the Cabinet Council had become entrenched at the epicenter of executive government. During Anne's reign (1702–1714) and early in George I's reign (1714–1727), members of Cabinet could be drawn from either of the two main political factions in Parliament, the Whigs or Tories.[2] ("Party" would be too strong a word for these groupings at that time.) From the time of Sir Robert Walpole's administration (1730–42), members of Cabinet generally all came from one faction or the other.

The Cabinet's executive powers legally derived from three sources: Orders in Council (addressed below); delegation by the monarch from his or her prerogative powers; and the powers attached to some of the ancient offices of State (such as that of Lord Chancellor: the holders of these offices of State were members of the Cabinet). The Cabinet was not a source of independent legal executive power; it was an administrative group with no distinct legal status.

George I was from Hanover (in modern Germany) and spoke little English when he became king in 1714. He did not frequently participate in Cabinet meetings. But first: how did he become king?

Queen Mary had died in 1694 at the age of thirty-two. She had not had a child. By 1700, her husband William was 50 years old and did not intend to remarry. Mary's sister Anne (the second child of James II) was 35 years old and childless. In that era, Anne's age and her tragic history of miscarriages and her children dying when young made it unlikely that she would produce an heir of her body. After William's death, she would succeed to the throne. But what would happen after Anne's death, or if she died before William? Disputed successions often ended in war. A Catholic successor would be a threat to the peace and security of England.

William and Parliament stepped up. Their primary objective was to ensure that the Crown passed from Anne to another Protestant. They wanted to adhere to the hereditary method of selection. The problem was that the strongest claimants on ordinary hereditary principles were all Catholics. William and Parliament departed from the usual hereditary order of succession and chose certain descendants of the eldest daughter of James I, Elizabeth Stuart. Those descendants were the ruling family of Hanover, an Electorate in the Germanic lands.[3]

How did Parliament square the circle and override the convention of inheritance by primogeniture?[4] By legislation. As we saw with some of the constitutional achievements of the English Revolution, the English constitution is not codified and can be modified by legislation. The ability to amend the English constitution by legislation is quite different from the usual position in countries which have a codified constitution—one written down in a single document (as amended). Codified constitutions usually require an amendment procedure which is more onerous than passing legislation, so they are harder to amend.

In the case of federal constitutions, the amendment procedures should protect the position of each of the federated states from the risk of expansion of the powers of the strongest states or the federal government. In the United States of America, Article V of the Constitution provides that an amendment is passed after it has been proposed by two-thirds of the members of each house of Congress (or by a constitutional convention) and ratified by three quarters of the State legislatures (or by State conventions).

The legislation which settled the succession after Anne was the "Act of Settlement." It was passed in 1701, some five years after the death of Queen Mary, when William was sole monarch and Anne was heir to the throne. It provided that The Princess Sophia, Electress of Hanover, and her Protestant heirs were to inherit after Princess Anne (later Queen Anne).

Sophia was the fifth daughter and twelfth child of Elizabeth Stuart, who was the eldest daughter of James I. Sophia had the misfortune to die less than two months before Queen Anne. Her heir George Louis, Elector of Hanover, succeeded Queen Anne as George I. It is through him that members of the current Royal Family have inherited the throne.[5] On ordinary principles of succession, he was probably fifty-sixth in line for the throne—but the first fifty-five were all Catholics. George succeeded to the throne in 1714.

It is not surprising that traditionalists found this dramatic departure from the conventional rules of inheritance a little hard to swallow. George was really a king by appointment, not by inheritance. That is one reason why some people joined the cause of the Stuart pretenders, James (son of James II) and Bonnie Prince Charlie (grandson of James II).

It was during the reign of George I that the function of a leading, or "first," or "prime" Minister developed. Sir Robert Walpole is generally considered to have been the first Prime Minister. The story of his career and administration is important for an understanding of the second phase of the development of modern executive government under the Westminster system (the phase from 1714 until the time of the great Parliamentary and other reforms of the 1830s), in which the Cabinet system continued but with the Prime Minister rather than the monarch playing the leading role.

As his father's eldest surviving son, Walpole inherited his family's estate in 1700, at the age of twenty-four. He increased his wealth by investing in the South Sea Company, which had a monopoly on English trade with Spanish America and was involved in financial schemes. He sold his shares before the notorious bursting of the "South Sea Bubble" of 1720. That event followed a frenzied speculative mania, caused partly by fraudulent directors and promoters of the Company's stock.

Walpole had been elected to the Commons in 1701. He was first appointed to an executive position in government in 1708, when he became Secretary of War. In 1715 he was appointed First Lord of the Treasury and Chancellor of the Exchequer, two of the most important offices in the British government.

The House of Commons formed a committee to investigate the circumstances of the South Sea Bubble. Based on the Committee's findings,[6] some of the directors and promoters of the South Sea Company were required to disgorge their profits, with the funds to be used to compensate victims of the crash. Walpole emerged unblemished from the Bubble.[7]

In April 1721 he was again appointed First Lord of the Treasury and Chancellor of the Exchequer, as well as Leader of the House of Commons. From this time, he was the principal Minister in the Government (the office called "Prime Minister" did not yet formally exist).

It has often been said that George I had little interest in the affairs of England, and was more concerned with foreign policy and the affairs of Hanover. This, it has been said, along with his lack of English, explained his decision to stop attending Cabinet meetings from 1717. But he and his ministers could all communicate in French, and by the later years of his reign he could clearly speak, read, and write English. So his lack of proficiency in English in the early years of his reign is a doubtful reason.

In Hanover, his powers were absolute. Yet there he allowed a relatively free press and granted sanctuary to the radical French writer and philosopher Voltaire, who was exiled from France. George was clearly liberal, at least by the standards of German princes. He was also financially prudent, which meant that he did not vex his subjects with excessive demands that they hand over their property to him as taxes. As we have seen, Crown demands for revenue and taxes had often been a source of conflict with Parliament.

His light-touch approach to government in England may have been an outcome of his judgement or wisdom to allow the English to use their institutions of government to govern themselves. His style certainly contributed to achieving what must have been his principal dynastic ambition: to consolidate his family on the throne of his unexpected new kingdom.

The Cabinet could not make an Order in Council unless the King was present. Such an order was required to implement many decisions with legal consequences; in contrast to administrative or policy decisions which did not need a decision with legal standing. Decisions of this latter type could be made by the Cabinet without the monarch. George attended meetings for the purposes of making Orders, but generally not otherwise.[8] If no Orders in Council were needed, the Cabinet could meet and report afterwards to the King on the outcome of its meeting. Minutes of Cabinet meetings were not kept, and what happened at its meetings was confidential.

Precisely when Walpole achieved such pre-eminence in Cabinet as to become the de facto Prime Minister is a matter of some debate and judgement. For years he worked closely with his Cabinet colleague Lord Townshend (Walpole's brother-in-law),[9] and the two of them were perceived to be the leading members of the Cabinet. Townshend's focus was particularly on foreign affairs. Townshend retired in 1730, and Walpole's ascendancy was complete. Walpole retired in 1742.

George I died and was succeeded by George II in 1727. Importantly for the continuing development of Cabinet government, the second George continued his father's practice of not attending Cabinet meetings.

Because the British constitution is not codified, it works partly through adherence to conventions. What is conventional can change over time. George I initially had the right to attend Cabinet meetings and to be the final decision-maker at them. As neither he nor George II did so, meant that the convention developed that the monarch would not attend Cabinet meetings or overturn Cabinet decisions.

Under the modern British system, the monarch appoints as Prime Minister the person who enjoys the confidence of the House of Commons—usually the Parliamentary leader of the majority party. The monarch then appoints Ministers from other members of Parliament chosen by the Prime Minister. The monarch does not seek to influence or interfere in either process. This all happens by convention.

There were six Prime Ministers in the first decade of George III's reign, from 1760 to 1770. He did not challenge the established principle that he could only obtain revenue for his Government with the approval of Parliament. But he could not find a Prime Minister who was able to retain the confidence of Parliament and with whom he could work successfully until Lord North (Prime Minister 1770–82), and then William Pitt the Younger[10] (first premiership, 1783–1801). An unwritten evolutionary constitution does not always work smoothly in the period when a new convention is being developed.

George III's churning of Prime Ministers early in his reign, along with his attempts to gain influence in Parliament by bestowing offices and using patronage, were interpreted in the North American colonies as a corruption of the British constitution as it had operated under Anne and especially under George I and George II.

This was a big deal in America, where there was both awareness of the extraordinary level of freedom that the free colonists enjoyed, and anxiety stemming from the colonists' lack of representation or influence in Britain to protect that freedom. Radical Whig political tracts were popular in America—they tended to emphasize the risk of George III being a more assertive monarch than his forebears. They looked back to the English Commonwealth and Protectorate when (as they told it) England had been governed by virtuous men with no monarch and looked forward to an idealized commonwealth republic where citizens would work for the common good, without pompous or inherited rank.

Anxiety can be compounded by poor communication. The Americans were dependent on sailing ships for their news and information from Britain, and had no direct representation in Parliament or in the British Government. George III came to be seen in America as a putative tyrant, and his behavior early in his reign made the risk of capricious or tyrannous government seem very real.

As noted above, during this second phase of the development of Cabinet government (1714 to 1830s) Parliament used its legislative power to pass statutes dealing with many specific executive matters. For example, the subject matter of the Acts passed in 1788 (the twenty-eighth year of George III's reign, and at the end of the American Revolutionary period) is instructive. This year has been chosen because it is approximately halfway through what I have called the second phase of development of Cabinet government.

Most of the Acts of 1788 are not "laws" in the sense of establishing enforceable and continuing rules. This is not to say that they were not valid Acts. They operated as authorizations and commands to the Government to do specific things, not as rules. To use my earlier description of the executive function, they deal with "doing things or getting the job done." By passing such Acts, Parliament was directly participating in the executive function of government.

Some Acts were concerned with specific national problems (such as the settling of American loyalists in Canada after the American Revolution), some were concerned with the general affairs of the Government (such as taxes and the appropriation of money for the Government's purposes), some were concerned with general trade issues. Many were concerned with specific individuals or specific programs—for example: the conduct of specific local infrastructure projects; the granting of annuities to specified individuals; the establishment of individual schools; and the building or repair of specific churches.

There were good constitutional and legal reasons why such specific individual and local issues needed to be addressed by Parliament. If taxpayers' money was to be spent for a specific purpose, the appropriation had to be approved by Parliament. If the Act altered property rights, such as by compelling the sale of land or the creation of easements or rights of way, legal authority was required.

The need for so many highly specific pieces of legislation declined with the later use of more comprehensive Acts authorizing revenue or expenditure, and the increased use of Acts delegating the power to make detailed rules to give effect to the objects of the Acts—so-called "subordinate legislation." The delegation was often to a member of the Government (commonly to the Minister who oversaw the relevant area of government), subject to oversight by Parliament. Subordinate legislation was not a legal innovation—the method had been used as early as the fourteenth century. But it was rarely used before the mid-nineteenth century.[11] It has been used with increasing frequency since then, as the scope and complexity of government has increased.

By the mid to late nineteenth century, many more general subjects were addressed in legislation—including the affairs of the British Empire and nature conservation—and fewer Acts were specific to an individual, a local building, or infrastructure programs. The scope of government had expanded, and Parliament was less occupied with the minutiae of government. Legislation was for the government of a vastly more modern country, with a more complex economy. By the mid-1800s, Parliament had become less active in passing executive statutes.

How and when did the mechanisms develop by which Parliament held the Cabinet and Government to account?

If a British Government suffers defeat in a no-confidence motion in the House of Commons, the Prime Minister and Ministers must resign, or Parliament will be dissolved and an election held. Before the development of Cabinet government, there were no no-confidence motions. As the monarch led the government before Walpole's time, a no-confidence motion would have been directed at the monarch personally and may have been treasonous.

The first vote which was interpreted as a no-confidence vote was in 1742. It brought down the first Prime Minister. There have been twenty-three no-confidence votes since then.[12] Five resulted in Parliament being dissolved and fresh elections being held. In the other cases, the Government resigned and was replaced by a new Government which enjoyed the confidence of the House of Commons.

The subject matter of the 1742 vote was not directly whether Walpole enjoyed the confidence of the House. His Government had introduced a petition against the return of two members of the House of Commons. The petition was defeated by one vote. Walpole considered that this meant that he had lost the confidence of the House. He resigned. Other members of Walpole's 1742 Cabinet did not resign—the principle of Cabinet solidarity had not yet been established. At the time of the next no-confidence vote, in 1782, all his Ministers resigned with Lord North.[13]

The two other main mechanisms by which modern Parliament can hold the Government to account are debates and votes on the legislation that the Government needs to support its administration and advance its policies, and question time.

What is question time, and how did it develop?[14] A Minister can be asked questions (orally or in writing) by other members of Parliament. Ministers are required to answer the questions put to them. The process is public, in that it occurs in Parliament in front of visiting members of the public. Questions and answers are published.

Questions can be friendly, giving Ministers an opportunity to advertise allegedly good work being carried out by the Government; neutral, seeking information or clarity about Government actions; or hostile, seeking to expose alleged misconduct or incompetence of the Government. Knowing that their work may be subject to public scrutiny in Question Time ought to help to ensure that both Ministers and the civil servants who assist them are less inclined to engage in behaviour which is in the interests of the Government or the State but not in the interests of the public.

The development of Question Time is an illustration of the organic development of conventions in the English constitution. It developed as Cabinet Government and the use of subordinate legislation developed. When the Government was actively led by the monarch, it would hardly have been seemly to invite His or Her Majesty to Parliament for the purpose of being interrogated by his or her subjects about the conduct of the Government. This would have debased the mystery and dignity of the Royal persona and function. It was unthinkable.

As executive government shifted from the King in Council to a Cabinet composed of Members of Parliament—and as Members of Parliament were accustomed to debating with and challenging one another—it was natural that Members outside the Ministry would ask Ministers, who were their Parliamentary colleagues, questions about what they were doing. The first such question was asked in 1721, when Earl Cowper asked the Government whether there was any truth in the report that the Chief Cashier of the South

Sea Company, Robert Knight, had fled the country and had been arrested in Brussels.

From Walpole's time, the Government needed to retain the confidence of the House of Commons. So, what could a Minister do when asked a question? To treat the questioner with contempt or disdain and expect to retain the confidence of the House would be reckless. Questions needed to be answered.

In the United States, Congress does not have question time with the President, and cannot vote him or her out of office with a no-confidence motion. This gives more scope for a President to play directly to his or her voter base, and to disregard the judgement and opinions of Congress and its members.

Walter Bagehot, the editor of "The Economist" magazine for seventeen years from 1861, wrote *The English Constitution*, a book published in 1867.[15] He described the operation of the British constitution as he saw it, and was not distracted by legal forms or by myths about how the constitution operated. He saw that England was by 1867 a disguised republic, with the monarch providing a dignified part of government, and the real work of government being done by the Cabinet and Ministry (what he called the "efficient part") supported by, and accountable to, the people's representatives in Parliament. Before the American Revolutionary period, Montesquieu had observed that if the monarch ceased to exercise the executive power, Britain would be a kind of republic.[16]

Bagehot also argued that to the extent that the British Government needs to pass legislation to implement its policies, the fact that the leaders of the executive (the Prime Minister and the members of the Cabinet) are chosen from Parliament and have the confidence of Parliament is helpful. The Government is likely to have the support of a majority of the legislators in implementing its program.

As we have seen, the most important legislation that a British Government needs to pass through Parliament is legislation authorising its revenue and appropriations (supply or "the budget"). A Government which fails to get its budget approved by Parliament will run out of money. The Government must then resign. Otherwise, in order to avoid a shutdown of government, the monarch must use the Crown's prerogative power to dismiss the Government or dissolve Parliament and call an election.[17]

There have been shutdowns of the United States' Federal Government's activities because of revenue or appropriations not being approved by one or both houses of Congress or by the President. The potential for shutdown is an example of the friction in the system of government established by the American Constitution, a consequence of the separation of powers and the Constitution's checks and balances. The checks can have cumbersome consequences. They were designed to prevent any one of the House, the Senate, or the President from being too dominant.

NOTES

1. The system of government of The United Kingdom of Great Britain and Northern Ireland, and of those places that have adopted the parliamentary systems based on it, including Canada, Australia, and New Zealand.

2. "Whig" came from "Whiggamore." The Whiggamores were west Scotland Presbyterians who marched on Edinburgh in 1648 to oppose Charles I. The Whigs tended to favor constraints on Royal power. "Tory" comes from Irish Celtic. It was a derogatory term for Irish Catholics who were dispossessed of their land as part of the suppression of Catholics and was applied to supporters of James II. They considered that his Catholicism should not make him ineligible. Tories tended to favor Royal power.

3. Its official name was the "Electorate of Hanover," because from 1708 the prince who ruled there was elevated to being one of the nine electors of the Holy Roman Emperor. Germany was not unified until the late nineteenth century, so "Germany" in reference to that period is a geographic and not a geopolitical term.

4. "Primogeniture" literally means by the first child but has come to mean by the eldest surviving son or his heirs.

5. German members of the Hanover/Windsor dynasty include George I and his wife, George II and his wife, George III's wife, George IV's first wife, William IV's wife, Victoria's husband Albert, and George V's wife. The Royal Family changed its family name from the German name of Victoria's husband (Saxe-Coburg-Gotha) to "Windsor" during World War I. Because the Germanic lands included many territories that were monarchies and Protestant, those lands provided the deepest reservoir of marriageable Protestant royals.

6. "The reports of the Committee of Secrecy to the Honourable House of Commons, relating to the late South-Sea directors, &c." Cato, London. Accessed September 2018. https://archive.org/details/pp1312061-2001/page/n0.

7. "Bubble Act 6 George I c18. 1719." Accessed October 2018. https://books.google.ca/books?id=BYlKAAAAYAAJ&lpg=PA372&ots=ujx1vUF28B&pg=PA322#v=onepage&q&f=false.

8. Technically Orders in Council were made by the Privy Council. They could however be made by the King with members of Cabinet who were Privy Councilors.

9. Townshend's descendants include both General Cornwallis, who commanded the British forces during the American Revolution, and Tommy Townshend, Lord Sydney, who was the Home Secretary responsible for the establishment of the first British colony in Australia, after whom the city of Sydney is named. Tommy Townshend chose for his barony the name Sydney in honor of his distant relative Algernon Sidney, the republican political theorist.

10. His father, also named William Pitt, had been Prime Minister.

11. Bourke, Stephen. 1991. "Subordinate Rule Making—An Historical Perspective." *Admin Review*, a newsletter of the Australian Administrative Review Council. Accessed October 2018. http://classic.austlii.edu.au/au/journals/AdminRw/1991/2 .pdf viewed and "Legislation of the United Kingdom: subordinate legislation." British Library. Accessed October 2018. https://www.bl.uk/voices-of-science/british library/~/media/subjects%20images/government%20publications/pdfs/subordinate -leg.

12. Counted in late 2018.

13. Since 2011, it has been a statutory requirement that if the House of Commons passes a resolution in the following terms, a parliamentary general election must be held: "That this House has no confidence in Her Majesty's Government."

14. "Factsheet P1 Parliamentary Questions." House of Commons Information Office. Accessed October 15, 2018 to July 2020. https://www.parliament.uk/documents /commons-information-office/p01.pdf.

15. Bagehot, Walter. 1878. *The English Constitution*. C. Kegan Paul & Co.

16. de Secondat, C. L., Baron de la Brede et de Montesquieu. 1748. *The Spirit of Laws*. Translated edition University of California Press, 1977, Book XI chapter 6 paragraph 45.

17. An Australian Prime Minister, E. G. Whitlam, in 1975 did not resign when Parliament had denied him supply. He was dismissed by the Governor-General (the Monarch's representative in Australia (which is a constitutional monarchy)) and lost the resulting general election in a landslide. English precedents may be distinguishable, because Whitlam was denied supply by the Senate and not by the lower house. Unlike the House of Lords but like the American Senate, the Australian Senate is an elected body and does have the power to block supply. At the time of his dismissal Whitlam still enjoyed the confidence of the lower house.

Chapter Five

British Coercion, American Resistance

The immediate cause of the American Revolution was the British policy in the 1760s and 1770s of trying to increase control over the British colonies in America. Boston was the place where that policy was most tested. Its economy was most dependent on shipping, so the end of the policy of "salutary neglect" affected it acutely. The colony had been founded by devout people in search of the freedom to govern themselves. Under Massachusetts' Charter of 1691, the colony had a higher degree of self-government than any colony other than Connecticut and Rhode Island, and its colonists expressly "have and enjoy all Libertyes and Immunities of Free and naturall Subjects . . . as if they and every of them were borne within [the] Realme of England . . ."[1]

The Seven Years' War of 1754–63 was on a larger scale than any of the three previous wars which had been fought between the British and French in North America. On the British side, those wars had been fought mainly by American colonists and their Native American allies. The War of 1754–63 required British troops and the Royal Navy.

In the eighteenth century, American settlement was moving westward. The charters of several colonies had claimed land extending from the Atlantic to the Pacific Ocean. But the French had claimed much of the same land. The French had explored, and established forts or trading posts from the Great Lakes southward, particularly down the valleys of the Mississippi and its tributary, the Ohio. In 1682 the French explorer La Salle claimed, in the name of the French Crown, all the basin of the Mississippi and its tributaries. New France included this huge territory, plus French Canada, which comprised much of modern southern Canada as far west as Fort Bourbon in Manitoba.

The War began in the upper Ohio valley in western Pennsylvania and what was then (but not now) north-western Virginia. The settler population of this part of the valley was principally British. The French ordered British settlers west of the Appalachian watershed to move out. They refused. The French captured or killed those settlers whom they could find.

In 1754 Virginia sent a force led by George Washington to establish a fort in the region (Fort Necessity, at modern Confluence, Pennsylvania). His force was substantially outnumbered, and he had to surrender the fort.

The French were successful for the first four years of the War.

Soon British troops, as well as the colonial militia, were fighting in America and the Royal Navy was blockading French supplies. William Pitt took control of the war effort in Britain. British victories on land began in 1758. In 1759 the Royal Navy had two substantial victories, in a battle off Lagos, Portugal, and at the decisive Battle of Quiberon Bay, off the south coast of Brittany, France. On land, the decisive British victory was at the Battle of Quebec in September 1759. Both the British and French commanders, Wolfe and Montcalm, were fatally wounded. Wolfe was immortalized as a British hero. In September 1760, the French surrendered Canada and all land east of the Mississippi to Britain ("except the town of New Orleans and the island in which it is situated . . .").[2]

In January 1760, Benjamin Franklin, the Pennsylvanian polymath, had written to Lord Kames, in terms consistent with his Albany Plan of 1754 (see chapter 7):

No one can rejoice more sincerely than I do [in the victory]; and this, not merely as I am a Colonist, but as I am a Briton. I have long been of Opinion that the Foundations of the future Grandeur and Stability of the British Empire lie in America, and tho', like other Foundations, they are low and little seen, they are nevertheless broad and Strong enough to support the greatest Political Structure Human Wisdom ever yet erected.[3]

But rather than victory leading to the British colonies in America becoming the heart of a greater British Empire built on a wise constitution, the War catalyzed the Empire's fracture and the birth of a great new republic.

George III's reign began in October 1760. He was saddled with the War and its enormous cost. British Government spending peaked in 1761 at £21.1 million. In that year total net income of the British Government was £9.6 million. By 1765 total British Government spending was down to £12 million, with defense spending of £5.9 million and interest on the national debt costing £4.83 million. But net income was only £10.9 million. British public debt increased from £72.2 million in 1754 to £133.6 million in 1765.[4] After the War, Britain kept ten thousand troops stationed in its newly conquered territory in North America at a cost of some £200,000 a year.

The proprietary and chartered company colony models enabled the colonies to be established at little cost to the Crown, and for private citizens to incur the costs and hardship of trying to build new businesses and communities in a remote and undeveloped land. It was a feature of this model that the Crown did not seek to directly tax its American subjects at normal rates. The colonists would contribute to Britain by the expansion of its territory and participation in the Navigation Act's system of a British monopoly on colonial trade and taxes on trade, not directly to British revenue.

The free colonists had control over their direct domestic taxes through their colonial representative assemblies and as members of councils that worked with their governors. The colonists' control of direct taxation was buttressed by the British constitutional principle of "no taxation without representation" which, as we saw in chapter 2, was at least as old as clause 14 of Magna Carta. Colonial taxes were used for paying the costs of the British administration in the colonies, and other purposes.

By 1714, British subjects in Britain were, on average, each paying ten times as much direct tax as subjects in the American colonies—5.4 times as much as those in Massachusetts, 18 times as much as those in Connecticut, 15.5 times as much as Virginians, and 35.8 times as much as Pennsylvanians.[5] And, as mentioned in chapter 1, the Americans had higher incomes. They were living in a land of immense opportunity for free colonists and, at the same time, enjoying the benefits of British colonial government and light direct taxes.

At the beginning of the War, the representative assemblies in Massachusetts and several other colonies refused to raise taxes or troops unless the assemblies, and not the royal governors, had control over military appointments and operations. Virginia's House of Burgesses preferred printing money and causing inflation to raising taxes.

The British Government wanted British Americans to bear a larger share of the tax burden. Viewed from Westminster, the huge increase in the cost of the national debt had been incurred largely for the benefit of the colonies. That assessment did not give the Americans credit for the militia and resources which they had contributed to the War, since those contributions were never reflected in Britain's financial accounts for the costs of the War.

The British Government's efforts to increase payments from the Americans included the Sugar Act of 1764, which sought to tax sugar and molasses imports from French and Dutch colonies. To try to end the widespread smuggling which had led to colonists evading the Molasses Act of 1733, the new Act included enhanced search and seize powers. Disputes about the operation of the Act had to be taken to the Vice-Admiralty Court in Halifax, Nova Scotia, not a colonial court with a jury sympathetic to local smugglers.

The Currency Act of 1764 was not a revenue raising measure. It was aimed at the colonies' printing of money rather than raising taxes to pay for their expenses. It did not ban local colonial currencies but did prohibit the colonies from using future issues of their local currencies for the payment of public or private debts.

The Stamp Act of 1765 required many printed materials (including legal documents, magazines, playing cards and newspapers) to bear a stamp issued by the Government. The stamp could only be bought with British currency. This was arguably a direct tax on the colonists, not a tax levied on traded goods. The colonists claimed that the Stamp Act was unconstitutional, as it imposed a direct tax without the approval of their representatives—there were no members of the House of Commons elected by Americans.

After strenuous protests from the colonists, and after they boycotted English goods, the Stamp Act was repealed in 1766. But to assert the right to tax, the Declaratory Act was passed at the time of the repeal of the Stamp Act. It was "declaratory" because it had no operative provisions—it merely asserted or declared a constitutional proposition: that the British Parliament "had hath, and of right ought to have, full power and authority to make laws and statutes of sufficient force and validity to bind the colonies and people of America . . . in all cases whatsoever . . ."[6] A face-saver for the British Government, but an inflammatory assertion in the colonies.

One of the arguments used by the Americans to resist the Stamp Act was reliance on the ancient principle of "no taxation without representation" (a principle popularized by the Boston lawyer James Otis). The British countered by saying that all British subjects were represented in the House of Commons: members of that House did not represent only the residents of their own electorates; they represented all British subjects. This theory of indirect representation was also used in Britain in defense of the hopelessly skewed electoral franchise, where major emerging towns and cities had no member of Parliament and, as we saw in chapter 3, rotten boroughs like Old Sarum did have members.

On the indirect representation theory, the Americans enjoyed "virtual representation" in the House just like the residents of places like Birmingham, England (which had no member of Parliament). The Americans maintained that it infringed the British constitution to purport to tax them when they did not have direct representation in the Commons. Their response to the Stamp Act included convening the First Congress of the American Colonies, at the instigation of the Massachusetts Assembly.

The purpose of the Congress was to "consult together on the present circumstances of the colonies." The Congress petitioned each of the King, the House of Lords, and the House of Commons. The fact that the colonies co-operated with one another and made joint petitions was momentous—the convening of subsequent congresses to co-ordinate opposition to the British would be a natural development.

The Congress' resolutions of October 19, 1765 included the following:

That His Majesty's liege subjects in these colonies, are entitled to all the inherent rights and liberties of his natural born subjects within the kingdom of Great-Britain.

That it is inseparably essential to the freedom of a people, and the undoubted right of Englishmen, that no taxes be imposed on them, but with their own consent, given personally, or by their representatives.

That the people of these colonies are not, and from their local circumstances cannot be, represented in the House of Commons in Great-Britain.

That the only representatives of the people of these colonies, are persons chosen therein by themselves, and that no taxes ever have been, or can be constitutionally imposed on them, but by their respective legislatures.[7]

The resolutions were lucid statements of the trans-Atlantic constitutional issues which drove the colonists to rebellion and revolution. Constitutionality was at the heart of the Americans' cause.

In 1766 a committee of the House of Commons questioned Benjamin Franklin about the American reaction to the Stamp Act. Franklin had been in London since December 1764 representing his home colony of Pennsylvania in the capital. His answers were a concise and lucid summary of American grievances and opinion while the Revolution was fomenting:

Q. Do you not know that the money arising from the stamps was all to be laid out in America?

A. I know it is appropriated by the Act to the American service; but it will be spent in the conquered Colonies, where the soldiers are; not in the Colonies that pay it.

Q. Do you think it right that America should be protected by this country and pay no part of the expense?

A. That is not the case. The Colonies raised, clothed, and paid, during the last war, near twenty-five thousand men, and spent many millions.

Q. Were you not reimbursed by Parliament?

A. We were only reimbursed what, in your opinion, we had advanced beyond our proportion, or beyond what might reasonably be expected from us; and it was a very small part of what we spent. Pennsylvania, in particular, disbursed about £500,000, and the reimbursements, in the whole, did not exceed £60,000.

Q. Do you not think the people of America would submit to pay the stamp duty if it was moderated?

A. No, never, unless compelled by force of arms.

Q. What was the temper of America toward Great Britain before the year 1763?

A. The best in the world. They submitted willingly to the government of the Crown, and paid, in their courts, obedience to acts of Parliament. Numerous as the people are in the several old provinces they cost you nothing in forts, citadels, garrisons, or armies, to keep them in subjection. They were governed by this country at the expense only of a little pen, ink, and paper; they were led by a thread. They had not only a respect but an affection for Great Britain; for its laws, its customs, and manners, and even a fondness for its fashions, that greatly increased the commerce. Natives of Britain were always treated with particular regard; to be an Old England-man was of itself a character of some respect, and gave a kind of rank among us.

Q. And what is their temper now?

A. Oh, very much altered!

Q. Did you ever hear the authority of Parliament to make laws for America questioned till lately?

A. The authority of Parliament was allowed to be valid in all laws, except such as should lay internal taxes. It was never disputed in laying duties to regulate commerce.

Q. In what light did the people of America use to consider the Parliament of Great Britain?

A. They considered the Parliament as the great bulwark and security of their liberties and privileges, and always spoke of it with the utmost respect and veneration. Arbitrary ministers, they thought, might possibly, at times, attempt to oppress them; but they relied on it, that the Parliament, on application, would always give redress . . .

Q. And have they not still the same respect for Parliament?

A. No; it is greatly lessened . . .[8]

So, no taxation without representation; only the local representative assemblies in America can represent and directly tax the American colonists; Parliament has abandoned its constitutional function of protecting British-American subjects from oppressive government; and the Americans had lost confidence in Parliament. An acute summary of why the Americans changed from being loyal subjects to rebellious defenders of their rights and liberties.

The British Government still needed revenue. British legislation known in America as the Townshend Acts was passed in 1767–68. Charles Townshend was the British Chancellor of the Exchequer. The Townshend Acts were structured, in accordance with established practice and consistently with

Franklin's comments to the Commons, not as direct or internal taxes but as taxes on traded goods or "duties to regulate commerce." The repeal of the Stamp Act and introduction of the Townshend Acts should have placated American opinion. It did not. Why?

One of the Acts was the Revenue Act of 1767. It imposed a duty on the importation of glass, lead, paints, paper, and tea. But it did not stop there. Americans acknowledged that taxes on trade were constitutionally valid, but they had a long history of smuggling to avoid them. The British Government included in the Act potent enforcement measures. These included authorising the use of "writs of assistance," a form of search and enforcement order which did not require the relevant goods or location of the search to be specified. Such writs were loathed in New England and had previously been the subject of celebrated legal cases there. The lawyer James Otis widely promoted his view that the writs were unconstitutional.

A proposed use of the new British revenue was to fund the salaries of the governor and colonial administrators. These costs had been paid from local taxes. The change was intended to increase the independence of administration from local influence. That change was not popular with the locals.

Two other Townshend Acts focused on enforcement measures. One established a new Customs Board, based in Boston, to drive more effective collection of duties on imported goods. As with the Sugar Act, jurisdiction for the enforcement of customs duties was moved from the colonial courts with trial by jury to the Vice-Admiralty Court. That Court was established in Boston, Philadelphia, and Charleston, as well as in Halifax.

The leaders of revolutionary movements often include some lawyers. By initially imposing constitutionally contentious taxes and then contentious enforcement procedures, the British Government was providing lawyers with arguments that the British were corrupting their own constitution and threatening the assured liberties of British Americans.

This had a dual effect on laying the road to American rebellion: it enabled the argument that rebellion was necessary to protect existing rights, and it corroded the emotional and sentimental bonds of the colonists to Britain. The narrative was that the corrupt and despotic administration of the mother country had betrayed the colonists, and that Americans rebelled to protect their constitutional rights.

How could the British Government have persuaded the Americans to bear their fair share of the Empire's expenses, at least those which had a direct or indirect benefit for the Americans? Perhaps the British could have allowed the Americans to choose, through an assembly in which they were directly represented, the extent of the Imperial support that they were prepared to pay for. That is a description of a loose British federation, and no-one was thinking of such an outcome in the 1760s.

The British Government lacked both sufficient political imagination and strategic awareness to develop a new constitutional framework for the colonists' existing partial independence. Only some people in Westminster understood that it would be impossible to bring the Americans back from the high-freedom, locally represented, low-tax model that had worked so well in establishing the colonies and had been allowed to persist for generations after that, to being treated more like subjects resident in the British Isles. Only some people in Westminster realized that attempted coercion would convince the Americans of the need for, and justice of, resistance, and that resistance could be successful for a people who were well established in and dispersed over an enormous area.

The Americans generally shared the view that was common among reformists in Europe, as well as in Britain and its American colonies, that the British constitution balanced the monarchical, aristocratic, and democratic elements of society, and resulted in liberty. For the Americans, the problem was not with the British constitution but with the British Government and its corruption of that constitution. This mindset was not conducive to thinking about radical alternative models for maintaining the relationship with Britain.

By the time the relationship between the thirteen colonies and the British Government had irretrievably broken down, a model such as forming a British federation would have been repulsive to both the Americans and the British. Federations probably need to be formed in amity, not in animosity. Most successful federations have been formed when separate political entities have agreed to a partial union, or in new settler territories; not as partial divorces of parts of a state or nation.

After the Townshend Acts, events led irremediably to revolt. In 1770, most of the Townshend duties were repealed to try to placate the colonists. But the colonists were implacable. Imposing on them measures which were unacceptable to them ratcheted up colonial antipathy. Withdrawing the measures after colonial opposition, several times over, taught the colonists the possibility of successful resistance. In Britain, the failure of concessions to calm the colonials was taken by some as evidence that concessions merely encouraged American insubordination.

A small duty on tea (first levied under the Revenue Act of 1767) was retained. The East India Company was given preferred access to the American market by the Tea Act of 1773. The Boston Tea Party (the dumping by colonists of 342 chests of East India Company tea in Boston harbor) and other riotous incidents followed.

Some British parliamentarians seemed to understand that, in dealing with the Americans, they were dealing with people who had a different political tradition, and that the consequences of strident policy might be disastrous. The majority took the position that the Americans must pay their taxes, and that their unruliness could not go unpunished. The failure of the previous concessions to the Americans made it likely that the hard men would gain the upper hand in determining British policy. They did.

In 1774, Parliament passed the four Acts which were known in America as the Coercive Acts, or the Intolerable Acts. Boston had been the center of the resistance to the change in British policy, so Boston was singled out for punishment under the Coercive Acts. The Acts included an Act which closed the port of Boston until compensation was paid for the Tea Party; the Massachusetts Government Act, which restricted town meetings in Massachusetts and abrogated the 1691 Charter; an Act which made British officials immune from prosecution in Massachusetts; and an Act which required colonists to house British troops who, in all the circumstances, were looking like an army of occupation.

When the British resorted to coercion after undermining the free colonists' long standing political and governance arrangements, they brought on the end game. If the British did not resort to violence, the colonies would be continuously rebellious. If they did use violence, the British would have both to hope that no enemy of Britain came to the colonists' aid, and to fund armies of occupation across a vast area occupied by colonists who considered that right was on their side.

Would the colonists dare to resist the British Empire? The colonists were a new breed of people, accustomed to a high level of independence and wary of any sign of tyranny from government. Some were descended from people of high conviction who had left Britain to establish liberty of worship in the wilderness. The colonists were highly literate and, at least on local and colonial issues, highly politically engaged. Their hearts and minds were not likely to be won back by coercion by people whom the Americans believed had betrayed their own constitution.

NOTES

1. ("Charter of Massachusetts Bay, 1691").
2. Article VII, the "Treaty of Paris 1763." The Avalon Project, Yale Law School. Accessed December 2018. https://avalon.law.yale.edu/subject_menus/constpap.asp.
3. "Letter from Benjamin Franklin to Lord Kames, 3 January 1760." National Archives. Accessed March 2019. https://founders.archives.gov/documents/Franklin/01-09-02-0002.

4. Tables 1, 2 and 7 Chapter XI, Mitchell, B. R. 1988. *British Historical Statistics*. Cambridge University Press.

5. Part III, Appendix A, (Rabushka 2008).

6. "The Declaratory Act, March 18, 1766." The Avalon Project, Yale Law School. Accessed April 2019. https://avalon.law.yale.edu/18th_century/declaratory _act_1766.asp.

7. "Resolutions of the Continental Congress October 19, 1765." The Avalon Project, Yale Law School. Accessed March 2019. https://avalon.law.yale.edu/18th_century /resolu65.asp.

8. ("Examination of Franklin before the Committee of the Whole of the House of Commons, 13 February 1766").

Chapter Six

The First American Constitutions

The State Constitutions

In May 1774 General Gage arrived in Boston as Governor of Massachusetts, appointed under the new Massachusetts Government Act. Gage was the commander-in-chief of British troops in North America. The British were determined "[to reduce the colony] to a state of obedience to lawful authority . . ."[1]

Massachusetts had had an elected council, an elected assembly, and substantial independence for six generations, since its Charter of 1629 (except for the period of the Dominion of New England from 1686 to 1691—see chapter 2). Its first English settlers had risked everything for freedom. Under its subsisting Charter of 1691 its citizens were assured of all English liberties. Now Massachusetts had as the head of its executive government a soldier whose job was to reduce it to obedience to Britain.

The Massachusetts Government Act also restricted public meetings, revoked those parts of the Charter of 1691 which provided for an elected council, and gave the Governor the power to appoint judges. The Act was based on a hope in Britain that stern measures and increased British Government control would bring the colonists to heel. The colonists believed that the repressive British measures were both unlawful and wrong in principle.

The Governor and Assembly relocated from Boston to Salem, because of the disturbances in Boston. Gage tried to prevent the Assembly from holding a valid meeting, so the elected members of the General Assembly moved from Salem to Concord and, on October 11, conducted themselves as an extralegal representative assembly: the Provincial Congress of Massachusetts.

Why were Massachusettsans prepared to convene a congress that had no legal status or authority? From their religious learning, the colonists were accustomed to the notion of a hierarchy of laws, with God's laws at the top. In the political realm, they were influenced by both the lessons from the history of the English revolutionary period in the previous century and the theories of

John Locke and other political philosophers. The colonists knew that Parliament had removed Charles I for ignoring Parliament's role; they knew of the circumstances and outcome of the English Revolution, and knew that their forebears had rebelled at the time of that Revolution (as we saw in chapter 2). They believed that if a Government acted unconstitutionally, its actions were not binding on British subjects.

That is an obvious notion now, but it was probably more well developed in eighteenth century America than anywhere else at the time. Americans had long experience of the risk to their freedom caused by the gap between their belief in their constitutional rights, and the governing class in England's changeable perception of those rights. The end of the policy of "salutary neglect" and the beginning of British coercion in the 1760s had focused the colonists' minds on that gap. And in New England, substantial independence from Britain was not just a political and cultural value but a necessary precondition for the colonists to be able to live a Godly life.

If the Parliament and Gage were acting unconstitutionally, the colonists believed that they were justified in establishing an alternative representative assembly. Submission to despotic or tyrannous government was the norm in most of the world. Even in England there was no Supreme Court that declared actions unconstitutional and specified the legal consequences. The Americans exercised self-help, to protect their exceptional rights as British subjects in the American colonies.

It would be easy to assume that the writings of a political philosopher like Locke were used after the event to justify revolutionary action but were too abstract or theoretical to really contribute to it. Yet in the lead-up to the Declaration of Independence in 1776, and throughout the revolutionary and constitution-writing period, key players used the language and theories of some political philosophers (Locke, Algernon Sidney, and Montesquieu in particular) in their explanations and communications. Some of the colonists were well versed in political and constitutional theory. Thomas Jefferson was famously a Lockean.

A common line of reasoning, based on social contract theory and Locke's version of it in particular, was as follows: individual people and families began as free agents in a "state of nature"; they agreed to form political societies for their mutual defense and benefit (the "social contract"); if the fundamental provisions of that social contract were breached by those people who were entrusted with government, the social contract would be dissolved and individual people and families would revert to a "state of nature"; and from the new "state of nature," they would be free to form a new social contract and system of government.

On this influential theory, a notion similar to constitutionality was at the foundation of the legitimacy of government. The theory also implied the sovereignty of the people.

What of the twelve colonies other than Massachusetts? From August 1774 (Virginia and North Carolina) to June 1776 (Pennsylvania), nine of the other colonies established new representative assemblies. It was not necessary to do so in Rhode Island, Connecticut, or Delaware because the governors in those colonies did not attempt to suppress or dissolve the existing assemblies.

In Virginia, when the House of Burgesses called for a day of prayer in response to the closure of Boston harbor pursuant to the coercive Boston Port Act, the Governor dissolved the House. The members of the House then convened as the First Convention and called for a congress of representatives of all the colonies.

The declaration of "The Association of the Virginia Convention" expressly declared recent Acts of the British Parliament to be unconstitutional and outlined the trade sanctions which the Virginians would impose on Britain— both a ban on imports and key exports. Any breach of the sanctions would be publicized, and the perpetrators would be "inimical to this country, and [we will] break off every connection and all dealings with them . . ."[2] Commercial and social ostracism would be used to enforce compliance with the decisions of the rebellious Convention.

The path to establishing the Provincial Congresses and other new representative assemblies, catalyzed by governors who dissolved or suspended the elected assemblies, was not only consistent with political theory, but it was also natural in the context of the colonists' practical experience of local representative government and the civil organization that they had already developed for the purpose of resisting British coercion since 1763.

Local government in the colonies had always been entirely in local hands. Town representative bodies had been established at the beginning of English settlement. In 1774, established town political organs were used to select delegates to county conventions. County conventions began to support the boycott of British goods and exercise police powers.

By 1774 the Massachusetts Committee of Correspondence was already two years old. It had been established at a Boston town meeting "to state the rights of the Colonists . . . and to communicate and publish the same to the several Towns in the Province and to the World."[3] The Committee also acquired and disseminated information and organized resistance to the British. Many Massachusettsan towns formed similar committees. The Massachusetts Committee was reconstituted in 1773 in response to a proposal from Virginia that all colonies establish committees with objects including liaising with committees in the other colonies and gathering and sharing intelligence.

By May 1774, all thirteen colonies had established committees for inter-colonial correspondence. This facilitated inter-colonial co-operation and made it easier to establish the First Continental Congress in September 1774.

As Governor Gage reported to Lord Dartmouth, Secretary of State for the Colonies, on September 25, 1774:

> Your lordship will know from various accounts, the extremities to which affairs are brought, and how this province [Massachusetts] is supported and abetted by others beyond the conception of most people, and foreseen by none. The disease was believed to have been confined to the town of Boston, from whence it might have been eradicated, no doubt, without a great deal of trouble, and it might have been the case some time ago; but now it is so universal, there is no knowing where to apply a remedy.[4]

The British attempt to bring the colonists to a state of obedience to British power was not going well.

The First Continental Congress was the second time that representatives of the colonies had met and determined on resistance to British measures (the first time had been the congress that resolved to oppose the Stamp Act). The Congress met in Philadelphia and issued two important documents. The "Declaration and Resolves" issued on October 14, 1774 established the legal and conceptual basis of the rebellion, and "The Articles of Association" outlined the practical steps which the Congress recommended to the colonies, to push on with the rebellion.

The "Declaration and Resolves"[5] was in three parts. The first part set out the context of the Declaration, by reciting the recent allegedly unconstitutional actions and other infringements of the British Government, and the authority and legitimacy of the Congress. The second part recited the rights of the colonists and the basis of constitutional British government in the colonies. It asserted that the colonists were "entitled to all the rights, liberties, and immunities of free and natural-born subjects, within the realm of England." (We saw in chapter 2 that Massachusetts' 1691 charter had conceded this principle: "[the colonists] have and enjoy all Libertyes and Immunities of Free and naturall Subjects . . . as if they and every of them were borne within this Our Realme of England.")

The Declaration described "the foundation of English liberty" and asserted that the colonists could not be adequately represented in the Commons, so that on most matters the representative colonial assemblies had exclusive legislative authority. It insisted on a right of freedom of assembly and a right to petition the King. It stated that a colony's consent was required before a standing army could be kept in the colony. And it asserted that members of a colonial council appointed by the Crown could not also act as legislators.

The articulation of rights in the Declaration in some places echoes the English Bill of Rights of 1689—a document with which many of the representatives at the Congress were familiar. The insistence on the Americans' rights within the English constitutional system is immensely important. This insistence asserted that it was the British who were acting unconstitutionally in oppressing British subjects in America—subjects who enjoyed British legal rights and British-American rights to limited self-government as a result of lawful grants and developments within the British legal system. In those circumstances, the British Government's action justified, or even necessitated, American resistance in order to protect existing rights.

The third part of the Declaration stated that specified recent British Acts of Parliament were "infringements and violations of the rights of the colonists" and that the repeal of those Acts was "essentially necessary, in order to restore harmony between Great Britain and the American colonies." This third part could be construed in Britain as an ultimatum.

Much of "The Articles of Association" is focused on trade sanctions, as was the declaration of The Association of the Virginia Convention. But, importantly, the Continental Congress' Articles served the additional function of being an agreement between the rebel colonies to form the Continental Association and to implement those sanctions. The Articles also called for the establishment of executive committees to conduct inspections and take enforcement action. This was a call for action, not just the assertion of a position. Rebel government was being established on the ground. The formation of the Continental Association was a step towards the formation of the United States.

Some members of Parliament in Britain understood that a British policy based on obtaining submission of the colonists by force, and the termination of the colonists' cherished independence and freedoms, would be calamitous. Foremost among them was William Pitt (Pitt the Elder), who had led the British war effort in the Seven Years' War of 1754–63 and seems to have understood that the Americans had political values and an experience of substantial independence that made them different from the King's subjects in the British Isles. Pitt admired the Americans. As he told the House of Lords[6] on January 20, 1775, while arguing for the withdrawal of troops from Boston:

> The Bostonians did not then complain upon slight, or temporary evil; but on an evil which sapped the very vitals of their constitution. . . . Full well I knew that the sons of ancestors, born under the same free constitution, and once breathing the same liberal air as Englishmen—ancestors, who even quitted this land of Liberty, the moment it became the land of Oppression, and, in resistance to bigotted [sic] councils and oppressive measures, tore themselves from their

dearest connexions; I say, my Lords, full well I knew that the offspring of such ancestors would resist upon the same principles, and on the same occasions.[7]

The conflict escalated. The first battles of Lexington and Concord occurred in April 1775. The rebels besieged Boston. In July 1775, the Second Continental Congress issued another Declaration: this time the "Declaration of the Causes and Necessity of Taking Up Arms."[8] It recited the justness of the Americans' cause, all the measures that they had taken to avoid violence, the aggression of Britain, and included the rallying cry: "Our cause is just. Our union is perfect. Our internal resources are great, and, if necessary, foreign assistance is undoubtedly attainable."[9]

In August 1775, George III issued a "Proclamation for Suppressing Rebellion and Sedition,"[10] which included an acknowledgement that the Colonies were in open rebellion:

> WHEREAS many of Our Subjects in divers Parts of Our Colonies and Plantations in North America, misled by dangerous and ill-designing Men, and forgetting the Allegiance which they owe to the Power that has protected and sustained them . . . have at length proceeded to an open and avowed Rebellion, by arraying themselves in hostile Manner to withstand the Execution of the Law, and traitorously preparing, ordering, and levying War against Us.

In June 1775, Congress had considered a request from the provincial congress of Massachusetts for advice on how it should establish civil government on a firmer legal basis. Congress was reluctant to recommend that the Massachusettsans draft a new constitution, because such a document would amount to an assertion of independence from Britain. Congress recommended that the Massachusettsans conduct themselves on the basis of that colony's Charter of 1691, which in the colonists' view had not been validly revoked.

In response to a similar request from New Hampshire, in November 1775 Congress went further and recommended that that colony have elected representatives work on a new constitution, which should lapse if peace was restored with Britain. In the same month, a request from South Carolina received the same response. And in December, Virginia's request also received that response. Constitution-making for the new America had begun. The colonists were preparing to formally secede from Britain and abolish their British colonial governments.

Meanwhile, in December 1775, the British "American Prohibitory Act" responded to the colonists' trade embargoes with Britain by instituting a general blockade on any trade with the rebellious colonies. Any vessels caught trading with the Americans would be forfeited to His Majesty as if they were enemy ships.

The first State constitution[11] is what you might expect in the circumstances. It was very short: some 940 words in total. It said nothing about the judicial or executive functions of government, and was focused on the legislative branch. It did not directly address the basis of sovereignty of the new State. It dealt with the exigencies of the moment, not political theory. It was adopted on the authority of the elected members of the Congress of New Hampshire.

This constitution noted that since the departure of the Governor, there was in effect no Government in New Hampshire, so that the Congress was acting to fill a dangerous void. It expressed a hope for reconciliation with Great Britain. It provided for an elected lower house of the legislature (the Representatives), and for an upper house of twelve (the Council) who would be elected by the electors in the several counties in New Hampshire. The Council would elect a President of the Council. Members of the Council had to own land. Public officeholders were to be appointed by the two Houses. Money or supply bills had to originate in the Representatives. Who could vote at elections was not mentioned, so the existing arrangement continued: legal free inhabitants paying taxes.

This first State constitution's emphasis on the legislature and failure to address the need for an executive branch of government are probably in part a legacy of the pre-eminence of the House of Commons in American thinking about the British constitution—the Commons being the body that asserted the ancient liberties of the English people, that challenged the tyrant Charles I, and whose status and functions had been enhanced by the English Revolution. The fact that the colonies had long had representative assemblies also made it natural to focus on the legislature.

The second State constitution, South Carolina's, was more considered.[12] It had a long preamble which recited the various British infringements and abuses and recited that there was currently an absence of effective civil government. It provided for two legislative chambers, an Assembly and a Council. The Council was to have a county franchise. Elections were to be held annually. The Assembly and Council were to appoint a President and commander-in-chief, and a vice-president. A privy council was to advise the President. The President had a veto power over proposed legislation. There were provisions dealing with the judiciary; and others dealing with the appointment of executive and military officers. Existing British laws and laws of the colony were to continue unless and until they were replaced with laws of the State.

On the question of sovereignty, South Carolina's constitution simply noted that the congress was invested with power to draft and adopt the new Constitution which implied, but did not expressly assert, the sovereignty of the people.

The third State constitution to be adopted was that of Virginia. The Virginians did not start work on their Constitution until May 15, 1776—although the Continental Congress had in December 1775 recommended that they do so. War with Britain had escalated in the intervening months. It is likely that in December some members of Virginia's provincial congress had still hoped to avoid a complete separation from Britain, but by May were convinced that Virginia needed a new State government.

General support for independence was pushed along by Thomas Paine's celebrated pamphlet *Common Sense*,[13] the most widely read and effective pamphlet published during the revolutionary period. It was first published in Philadelphia in January 1776. Paine did not just assertively argue for independence on the basis that the British had oppressed and gone to war with the colonists. Showing no deference, he argued that the famed balanced British constitution was two parts (the monarchy and the Lords) tyrannous, that American independence was inevitable, and that the Americans should seize the opportunity to establish a republic on a footing that would ensure their liberty and prosperity. He cast a harsh light on the habitual or sentimental aspect of Americans' attachment to Britain.

The Virginian Constitution, adopted in June 1776,[14] included three novel features of great significance:

- a Declaration of Rights;
- a statement of the sovereignty of the people; and
- an express statement that there were three separate functional "departments" of government (legislative, executive, and judicial) which must be kept "separate and distinct," so that none purported to exercise the powers of another and so that no person could participate in more than one at the same time.

This Constitution did not merely set out the practical provisions required for effective independent government. It described a new type of government with the free individual at its heart, combining with other individuals to establish government for the protection of their liberty, and limiting the operation of the different branches of that government in order to constrain the corrosive and corrupting influence of political power.

It was the best of Britain, and the theories of Locke and Montesquieu, made real. It described a sound theoretical basis of a new system of government and it established the rules for the machinery of government that would give life to that theory, all built on free people, whose continuing freedom from oppression was assured.

With this document, the American rebellion became a revolution. A revolution of a very specific type. Americans did not remake their society. They exited the British Empire and protected the liberties that Britain had enabled but then sought to crush. As with the two previous State constitutions and all those that followed, the British legal system based on common law was to continue. The American revolution was a revolution of political theory and organs of government, not a revolution of law or legal system. The crisis with Britain that began in 1763 had focused the minds of many leading colonists on constitutional issues, and by 1776 the Virginians had many of the answers to what was required to protect their liberties and establish an independent system of government without a monarch.

The rights set out in the Declaration of Rights were "the basis and foundation of government." It was implied that laws could not be inconsistent with these foundational rights. The rights were grounded in the English Bill of Rights but were modernised and more extensive. Some of the "rights" were potentially legally enforceable individual or general protections such as:

- the right to the enjoyment of life and liberty, with the means of acquiring and possessing property, and pursuing and obtaining happiness and safety;
- the right to a fair trial by jury;
- the right to vote;[15]
- the right to freedom of religion; and
- a guarantee of freedom of the press.

Other "rights" were declarations of the foundations of the new system of government or general principles of government, including that:

- (as noted) the three branches of government must be kept separate;
- all power was vested in, and consequently derived from, the people; and
- if and when government was inadequate for or acting contrary to its proper purposes, the majority of the population could alter or abolish it.

Some other "rights" described important but more mechanical aspects of government.

Article 15 did not fit into any of these categories. It was more an exhortation to virtuous republican citizenship: "That no free government, or the blessings of liberty, can be preserved to any people but by a firm adherence to justice, moderation, temperance, frugality, and virtue, and by frequent recurrence to fundamental principles."

That a democracy might deteriorate to mob rule, or that the majority oppress the minority, had been understood as a risk since the days of Plato and Aristotle. These ancient Greek philosophers had noted that the practice of civic virtue—or limiting the voting franchise to virtuous citizens—might be needed to avoid such an outcome. George Mason, the principal author of the

Declaration of Rights, hoped for a polity of virtuous citizens. The voting franchise in late colonial and revolutionary America used as its selection criteria: age, legal status (free or not free), race (in many but not all States), gender, and possessing an interest in property.

The Virginian Constitution recited the various abuses committed by the British, and stated the practical necessity of speedily adopting a "regular adequate Mode of civil Polity . . . in Compliance with a Recommendation of the General Congress." Much of this Constitution deals with the establishment of the new legislature. The executive was to be constrained, with no veto and one-year terms for the governor. The governor was to be chosen by a joint vote of the House of Delegates and the Senate.

New Jersey adopted a State Constitution two days before the Declaration of Independence. It drew on the earlier State constitutions and contained one innovation. Its final clause, clause XXIII, required each elected representative to take a personal oath not to interfere with the frequency of elections, the right to jury trial, or with freedom of religion. They were also to swear not to injure the public welfare. The requirement for this oath was an attempted solution to the problems of how to entrench fundamental rights and of the potential for the corruption of legislators.

Some later State constitutions followed New Jersey in requiring a personal oath as a mechanism for requiring a commitment to the new constitutional arrangements. The final American Constitution famously requires the President to swear that "I will to the best of my Ability, preserve, protect and defend the Constitution of the United States." It also requires all members of Congress and all holders of executive or judicial office to swear to support the Constitution.

And so, to the Declaration of Independence. To read it is to be in awe: at the audacity of its purpose; at the idealism of its vision; and at the beauty of its prose. By this document Americans unfriended George III and unlawfully seceded from Britain. They declared their colonies to be sovereign States. The States were to be united.

The actual declaration of independence is in the final paragraph of the document:

> We, therefore, the representatives of the United States of America, in General Congress assembled, appealing to the Supreme Judge of the world for the rectitude of our intentions, do, in the name and by the authority of the good people of these colonies solemnly publish and *declare, That these United Colonies are, and of right ought to be, FREE AND INDEPENDENT STATES; that they are absolved from all allegiance to the British crown and that all political connection between them and the state of Great Britain is, and ought to be, totally dissolved* [emphasis added].[16]

The most famous parts of the Declaration are not the assertion of independence, but its statement of principles near the beginning:

> We hold these truths to be self-evident: That all men are created equal; that they are endowed by their Creator with certain unalienable rights; that among these are life, liberty, and the pursuit of happiness; that, to secure these rights, governments are instituted among men, deriving their just powers from the consent of the governed . . .

and its Lockean statement of the circumstances in which rebellion is justified, which immediately follows the statement of principles:

> . . . [and] that whenever any form of government becomes destructive of these ends, it is the right of the people to alter or to abolish it, and to institute new government, laying its foundation on such principles, and organizing its powers in such form, as to them shall seem most likely to effect their safety and happiness . . .

A committee of five had been appointed by the Second Continental Congress to write the Declaration. The five were Benjamin Franklin, Thomas Jefferson, John Adams, Robert Livingston, and Roger Sherman. Thomas Jefferson wrote the draft, which the Committee did not substantially amend. The declaration draws heavily on the Virginian Declaration of rights which, as noted above, is principally attributed to George Mason.

The Declaration is grounded in social contract theory, described earlier in this chapter—both the process of forming government ("the right of the people to . . . institute new government") and the process of terminating governments or systems of government ("the right of the people to alter or abolish it"). The Declaration's preamble also refers to the violation of natural law, which is more fundamental than other laws, as justifying secession: ". . . it becomes necessary for one people to dissolve the political bands which have connected them with another, and to assume . . . *the separate and equal station to which the laws of nature and of nature's God entitle them* . . . [emphasis added]." (As we saw in chapter 2, in January 1689 the Convention Parliament had referred to both a social contract and natural law when it resolved that James II had "[broken] the Original Contract between King and People; and . . .violated the fundamental Laws . . .")

The statements "That all men are created equal; that they are endowed by their Creator with certain unalienable rights" had moral, political and legal dimensions. In the Virginian Declaration, the corresponding words had been: "That all men are by nature equally free and independent, and have certain inherent rights . . ."

Where did the notions that all men are created equal, and that all men have unalienable rights, come from?

Before answering that question, a note on the meaning of "men" in this phrase. Slaves did not have the legal, civil, or political rights of free people. The inconsistency of the statements about equality and rights with the position of slaves troubled many Americans, especially in the North but also at least as far south as Virginia. Slavery was, however, widely believed to be necessary for the plantation economy of the South. It would have been politically and economically impossible to abolish slavery in the middle of the rebellion against Britain.

The members of the drafting committee, and the Congress generally, were too well steeped in Christian moral teaching and the writings of the Enlightenment political philosophers to leave out the equality statement. The statement was one of deep conviction but also, no doubt, of political utility in emphasising the moral and social difference between the new system and the British colonial system. The contradiction between that conviction and the continuance of slavery was real. It was not a product of the Declaration but was reflected in it.

And what about women? "Man" and "men" are, and especially were until recently, terms with at least two meanings. They were widely used to mean "mankind," a term describing the human species. In other contexts, "man" and "men" mean a member or members of the male sex only. Male slaves had no political and few legal rights, and non-slave males did not have equal political rights. For example, not all free men had the right to vote as there were property and residency requirements in most States. Free women had few political rights at the time, but most of the legal protections that free men enjoyed. The generally stated reason for the limited political rights of both free women and free unpropertied men was the same, that women and such men lacked experience in worldly and political matters and were likely to have their opinions in those matters determined by others. Free African Americans were denied the vote in many colonies, a form of racial discrimination not related to being unfree.[17]

"Men" in the Declaration seems to have meant mankind, but the equality and unalienable rights statements were subject to exclusions, described above, that were customary at the time. Yet the boldness and aspiration of the statements, and their appeal to divine origins—"That all men are created equal; that they are endowed by their Creator with certain unalienable rights"—invites the question: were the customary exclusions morally right? The unqualified language of the statements of course provided the civil rights movement with a powerful argument: the statements were meant as written. Dr. Martin Luther King, Jr. was to draw on the statements in his compelling and uber-famous "I Have A Dream" speech in 1963: "This . . . was a promise that all men—yes, black men as well as white men—would be guaranteed the unalienable rights of life, liberty and the pursuit of happiness."[18]

King's speech was imperative and momentous, partly because it was grounded in abuse, suffering and heroism; partly because of its ethics, imagery and prose; and also, because it interpreted the conviction of the Declaration as being universal, without contamination by social conventions or customary exclusions.

Back to the question: where did the notions that all men are created equal, and that all men have unalienable rights, come from?

Most immediately, from the Enlightenment political philosophers including Locke and Montesquieu. Their work included an emphasis on political participation by much of the population in a free society. Many of the leading American revolutionaries had read at least some of the work of these philosophers.

But do not forget the role of the British constitution itself. Before the Americans gave up on the possibility of reconciliation with Britain, they were constantly reminding the British of the Americans' political rights (and the way in which the British had since 1763 abused those rights). The Americans admired the British constitution but deplored the recent British ministries or governments. A second major source of the unalienable rights statement (but not the equality statement) was the American understanding of the British constitution and legal system.

Larry Siedentop, in his book *Inventing the Individual* argues that Christianity (because of its teaching that each individual, regardless of their social or economic position, is of equal moral value and has a direct personal relationship with God) and thinkers of the Middle Ages laid the basis for all this: "We have found that a 'deep' foundation for the individual [as opposed to the family or tribe] as the organising social role—a status which broke the chains of family and caste—was laid by lawyers, theologians, and philosophers from the twelfth to the fifteenth century."[19]

The first State constitution adopted after the Declaration, on September 21, 1776, was that of Delaware. A convention was elected for the purposes of drafting and adopting a declaration of rights and a constitution for the independent State. The Constitution applied the New Jersey innovation by requiring its legislators to swear an oath of submission to its constitution and laws. It also provided for a right of appeal in legal disputes to a court comprising the State President and six elected legislators, a system based on the right of appeal in Britain to the House of Lords. Slaves could not be brought into the State for sale.

In Pennsylvania, a convention was also elected. It convened on July 15, and adopted a declaration of rights and a constitution, which were signed by Benjamin Franklin as President of the Convention on September 28, 1776. It was the most radically democratic of the State constitutions. Its declaration of rights drew on Virginia's. The Constitution provided for a single elected legislative chamber, and for an elected executive council to assist the elected president. Members of the House of Representatives were to be elected annually. A record of proceedings of the House was to be printed weekly. Proposed laws would generally not come into effect until the session of the House after the session in which they were last read for debate and amendment.

Maryland was next. It also elected a convention for the task. The Maryland Constitution was adopted by the convention on November 8.[20] It provided for a legislature with two houses, a House of Delegates, and a Senate. It did not contain any innovations. Its Declaration of Rights, adopted on November 3, had a staggering forty-two clauses, and was almost 2,500 words in length. Some of the clauses describe fundamental individual rights, mostly derived from the Virginian Declaration of Rights, but many clauses describe other matters, such as:

- a theory of sovereignty ("That all government of right originates from the people, is founded in compact only, and instituted solely for the good of the whole."), and other political theories;
- procedural requirements, such as where the legislature should sit and how petitions could be brought; and
- principles for the selection and duration of the terms of judges and other officials in office.

From May 11, North Carolina had been governed by a council of safety. On October 15, elections were held for a representative assembly which would act as a legislature, and both draft and adopt a constitution. That assembly adopted a constitution on December 14 and a declaration of rights on December 17. The Constitution contained no material innovations, other than prohibiting any clergyman or preacher from holding office as a member of the State's Senate, House of Commons, or Council of State. This demonstrated a determination to keep religion out of government. Immigrants to North Carolina were of German, Swiss, Irish, and Scottish descent as well as from England and from British colonies. Many had different churches, and the State wanted more immigrants, so it was desirable not to allow any religious denomination to gain influence in government.

Then came Georgia. As in North Carolina, elections were held for a representative assembly which would act as a legislature, and both draft and adopt a constitution. Like Pennsylvania, Georgia was to have one elected legislative chamber and an elected executive council. Elections were to be annual. Free African American men who met the property qualification for voting could not vote. This Constitution had no separate declaration of rights, although many rights were included in the provisions of the Constitution which dealt with the judicial system. The Constitution was adopted on February 5, 1777.

New York's new Constitution was not adopted until April 20, 1777. On May 10, 1776, the Continental Congress had resolved:

> That it be recommended to the respective assemblies and conventions of the United Colonies, where no government sufficient to the exigencies of their affairs have been hitherto established, to adopt such government as shall, in the opinion of the representatives of the people, best conduce to the happiness and safety of their constituents in particular, and America in general.[21]

New York's Gouverneur Morris had proposed on May 24, 1776 that the colony act on this resolution. A new congress was elected which, as in North Carolina and Georgia, would act as a legislature and both draft and adopt a constitution. It first met on July 9, 1776. A draft Constitution was not submitted to it until March 12, 1777. The delay was at least in part attributable to the disruption caused by the British occupation of parts of New York, and to the War, which included battles at Harlem Heights on September 16, White Plains on October 28, and Fort Washington on November 16, 1776.

The New York Constitution had one novel feature. It had been widely said of the British constitution that it perfectly combined the benefits of monarchical, aristocratic, and democratic influence. As noted above, one of the theoretical risks faced with the new American constitutions was that they might lead to oppression by the majority, or to legislation that was for other reasons unwise.

The New York Constitution of 1777[22] noted that "laws inconsistent with the spirit of this constitution, or with the public good, may be hastily and unadvisedly passed" and provided that a council comprising the Governor, Chancellor, and judges of the supreme court (or any two of them) could review proposed laws which had passed through the legislature and recommend changes. The senate and house of assembly could accept any recommendations or reject them by a two-thirds majority. The Council of Revision was to object to 128 proposed pieces of legislation, of which seventeen were passed notwithstanding the objections.[23] As we shall see in chapter 8, the Virginia Plan for the Constitution of the United States included a proposed Council of Revision.

Massachusetts was proceeding on the basis that its Charter of 1691 had not been validly revoked. A similar position pertained in Connecticut and Rhode

Island. The general assembly of Rhode Island resolved in May 1776 to re-place all references to the king in official documents, implying that the 1663 Charter still applied, but in republican form. In October 1776, the general assembly of Connecticut confirmed that its 1662 Charter was still in effect.

The Massachusettsans' constitutional position was problematic. As the grantor of their Charter (the English monarch) had purported to revoke it, a new constitution was required. In 1776 the towns refused to authorise the General Court (the elected legislature) to draft and approve a new consti-tution. A constitutional convention was considered but rejected. A newly elected house of representatives met in June 1777 which was specifically authorised to draft a constitution. The resulting document was rejected in a general poll in 1778.

A constitutional convention was then elected and met in Cambridge in September 1779. John Adams was the principal author of the draft that it produced. His draft declaration of rights and constitution were accepted by the convention on March 2, 1780, with some changes. It was put to a popular vote, approved, and came into effect on October 25, 1780.[24]

We are all fortunate that John Adams did not hold the pen in drafting the Declaration of Independence or the final Federal Constitution. A future Presi-dent, he was a man of immense knowledge of political theory and history, but his constitution for the State of Massachusetts included many statements of theory, mini-preambles, and contextualising statements. His "Part the First" was a wordy declaration of rights, running to thirty clauses. Habeas corpus, one of the most fundamental rights, is not dealt with in the declaration of rights, but in chapter VI of the document.

We have seen that the Virginian Declaration of Rights contained an exhor-tation to virtuous citizenship. The Massachusettsan Constitution had an entire operative chapter devoted to the development of Harvard College and another (chapter VI) devoted to "the duty of legislatures and magistrates" to take steps to nurture the development and diffusion of knowledge and "to coun-tenance and inculcate the principles of humanity and general benevolence, public and private charity, industry and frugality, honesty and punctuality in their dealings; sincerity, and good humor, and all social affections and gener-ous sentiments, among the people."

Knowledge and virtue were necessary to the success of republican govern-ment, but also to be pursued for their own sake. The idealism that motivated many of its leaders is one of the aspects of the Revolutionary period which makes it so enchanting.

This Constitution gave the Governor a right to review and object to pro-posed legislation, similar to the Council of Revision's power in the New York constitution. The Governor, Senators and members of the House of Representatives were to be elected annually. Candidacy for office and the right to vote were subject to property qualifications.

Until New Hampshire's State Constitution, there were no American constitutions, only some British charters. By the end of October 1780, eleven States[25] had new constitutions, all based on the sovereignty of their citizens. The continuation of the common law, and a separation of powers between frequently elected representative assemblies; weak executives; and independent judiciaries, were common features of these radical new arrangements.

Before independence, some of the revolutionary leaders had acquired a profound knowledge of the history and theory of political science. Now the theory was being trialled.

At least with the State constitutions, the dimensions of the challenge were obvious: to progress from British colonies to independent republics with comprehensive representative governments, elected by eligible citizens.

There was another massive and imperative challenge: to what extent would these independent republics co-operate with one another? And how would they organise that co-operation? A limited arrangement for mutual defence only? Surely not a national Government, with the risk of substituting the oppressive British Government with a new tyranny? While the required scope of the State constitutions was clear, both the scope and form of any co-operative arrangement that transcended the States were open questions. The Constitution of the United States of America was not the immediate answer.

NOTES

1. "Letter from the Earl of Dartmouth, Secretary of State for the Colonies, to the Hon. Governor Gage, Whitehall, April 9, 1774" in *The Parliamentary History of England, from the earliest period to the year 1803* Volume 18 (London: T. C. Hansard, 1813), 75–7. Accessed Hathi Trust Digital Library January 2019. https://babel .hathitrust.org/cgi/pt?id=umn.31951d01078685f&view=1up&seq=59.

2. "Resolutions of the Virginia Convention, August 1–6, 1774." The Avalon Project, Yale Law School. Accessed March 2019. https://avalon.law.yale.edu/18th_century /assoc_of_va_conv_1774.asp.

3. "Manuscript copy of the minutes of the first meeting of the Boston on Committee of Correspondence, Nov. 3, 1772." Collection of the New York Public Library. Accessed February 2019. https://www.nypl.org/blog/2015/11/30/boston-committee -documents.

4. "Letter from Lord Dartmouth to Governor Gage lamenting the behaviour of the House of Representatives and the mob, August 3, 1774." University of Chicago Library, from the National Archives. Accessed January 2019. http://pi.lib.uchicago .edu/1001/cat/bib/11585240.

5. "Declaration and Resolves of the First Continental Congress, October 14, 1774." The Avalon Project, Yale Law School. Accessed November 2018 to July 2020. https://avalon.law.yale.edu/18th_century/resolves.asp.

6. Pitt was by then the Earl of Chatham and sat in the House of Lords.

7. "The Speech Of the Right Honorable The Earl of Chatham, In the House of Lords, Jan. 20, 1775." Evans American Early Imprint Collection, University of Michigan Library. Accessed September 2018 to July 2020. https://quod.lib.umich.edu/e/evans/N11390.0001.001?rgn=main;view=fulltext.

8. "Declaration by the Representatives of the United Colonies of North-America, Now Met in Congress at Philadelphia, Setting Forth the Causes and Necessity of Their Taking Up Arms." p. 168, Morison, Samuel Eliot and Henry Steele Commager, William E. Leuchtenburg. *The Growth of the American Republic*: Volume 1. Seventh Edition. New York: Oxford University Press; 1980. Accessed August 2018 to July 2020. The Avalon Project, Yale Law School https://avalon.law.yale.edu/18th_century/arms.asp.

9. Why did the revolutionary leaders write so well, in such rousing and compelling prose? The book with which most colonists were intensely familiar was the King James Version of the Bible, and it was written in beautiful prose and poetry, to be read aloud. Its rhythms and cadences can even now be heard in American political oratory, including some of the speeches of candidate and then President Obama. See generally (Bragg 2012).

10. "Proclamation, For Suppressing Rebellion and Sedition" August 23, 1776. National Archives. Accessed November 2018 to July 2020. https://www.archives.gov/historical-docs/todays-doc/?dod-date=823.

11. Wood, Gordon S. 1969, *The Creation of the American Republic*, The University of North Carolina Press, is one of the most important books on the writing of American constitutions. Its contributions include that it focusses attention on the importance of the first Constitutions, the State Constitutions.

12. New Hampshire and South Carolina both replaced their initial constitutions before the American Constitution became operative, in 1784 and 1778, respectively.

13. Paine, Thomas. 1776. *Common Sense: addressed to the Inhabitants of America*. R, Bell, Philadelphia.

14. "Constitution of Virginia, June 29, 1776." The Avalon Project at Yale Law School, but diverted to George Mason University's Aontonin Scalia Law School's website. Accessed October 2018 to July 2020. https://www.law.gmu.edu/assets/files/academics/founders/VA-Constitution.pdf.

15. This right was to be enjoyed by "all men, having sufficient evidence of permanent common interest with, and attachment to, the community," language which was understood to mean free white men who satisfied a property qualification.

16. ("Declaration of Independence" 1776).

17. Under the final Constitution, determining who could vote and the boundaries of electoral districts was left to the States. Certain State restrictions on the right to vote later became unlawful as a result of amendments to the Constitution: the Fifteenth Amendment (voting franchise could not be limited by race, color, or previous

condition of servitude), the Nineteenth Amendment (women's right to vote), and the Twenty-Sixth Amendment (which lowered the voting age to 18).

18. King, Jr., Dr. Martin Luther. 1963. "I Have A Dream" speech. Accessed March 2019 to July 2020. https://ourlutherking.com/i-have-a-dream-speech-text/.

19. Siedentop, Larry. 2014. *Inventing the Individual: the origins of Western Liberalism*. Allen Lane, page 338.

20. "A Declaration of Rights, and the Constitution and Form of Government agreed to by the Delegates of Maryland, in Free and Full Convention Assembled," November 1776. The Avalon Project, Yale Law School. Accessed November 2018 to May 2020. https://avalon.law.yale.edu/17th_century/ma02.asp.

21. *Journals of the Continental Congress*, May 10, 1776. Volume 4. Library of Congress, 1906, Hathi Trust Digital Library, page 342. Accessed October 2018 to July 2020. https://babel.hathitrust.org/cgi/pt?id=hvd.32044020407417&view=1up &seq=348.

22. "Constitution of New York, 1777." The Avalon Project, Yale Law School. Accessed October 2018 to July 2020. https://avalon.law.yale.edu/18th_century/ny01.asp.

23. Footnote 2 to The Avalon Project's copy of the Constitution of New York, citing Hough, which is a reference to an unidentified work of Franklin Benjamin Hough.

24. "Constitution of Massachusetts, 1780." George Mason University, Antonin Scalia Law School. Accessed July 2019. https://www.law.gmu.edu/assets/files/aca demics/founders/Mass-Constitution.pdf.

25. The position in Vermont is not considered in this book because it was not one of the thirteen founding States.

Chapter Seven

The Confederation Was Not Enough

While the State Constitutions were being drafted and adopted, the War of Independence continued, year after year.[1] For much of the War, the Americans were losing the battles or unable to even take the field because of the pitiful condition of their armies.

The urgent tasks of raising, supplying, and deploying American military forces and of seeking support from Britain's enemies, required substantial co-operation between the Colonies (and after the Declaration, the States). By necessity, the Continental Congress played a leading role in co-ordinating the American forces. But it had no defined powers and little executive capacity. Sustained co-operation required an agreed structure and terms.

The Continental Congress on July 21, 1775 considered rough draft Articles of Confederation, drafted by Benjamin Franklin, for "the United Colonies of North America" ("Colonies" because independence had not yet been declared).

Franklin had been thinking about inter-colonial co-operation for years. In 1754, during the Seven Years' War, he had authored the Albany Plan[2] for "one general government" which proposed that the Colonies would grant specified powers to a general government. It was a plan for greater American autonomy within the British Empire. Under that Plan, a general government would have controlled dealings with the Native American nations and have raised military forces for the defence of the Colonies. It would have had power to raise revenue by taxation. The head of the executive branch would have been a President-General, appointed by the British government. There would have been a "Grand Council, to be chosen by the representatives of the people of the several Colonies met in their respective assemblies . . ." The Plan was considered at the Albany Congress in 1754 but rejected by both the British and by the Colonies.

On June 12, 1776, the day after appointing a committee to draft a declaration of independence, the Continental Congress appointed a committee to draft articles of confederation. The committee was chaired by John Dickinson. The draft Articles were presented to Congress on July 12.[3] They were debated and amended for more than a year and adopted by the Continental Congress on November 15, 1777.[4] The States then generally acted as though the Articles were in force, although the Articles did not formally come into effect until they were ratified by all thirteen States, which occurred when Maryland ratified on March 1, 1781.[5]

As we will see, the Confederation was to fail because it lacked sufficient power and enforcement mechanisms. America needed more than a forum in which the States could co-operate if they chose to do so. But without the failure of the Confederation, Americans would probably not have been prepared to adopt the more potent federal and national government created by the final Constitution. The Confederation was a necessary step on the path to the Constitution and nationhood.

Article III provided that: "The said States hereby severally enter into a firm league of friendship with each other." Contrast this insipid language with the imperative conviction of the following words from the Declaration: "That all men are created equal; that they are endowed by their Creator with certain unalienable rights; that among these are life, liberty, and the pursuit of happiness" and these words from the Constitution: "We, the people of the United States, in order to form a more perfect Union, establish justice, insure domestic tranquillity, provide for the common defense, promote the general welfare, and secure the blessings of liberty to ourselves and our posterity, do ordain and establish this Constitution for the United States of America."

The language of the Declaration and the Constitution compel a visceral response from the reader or listener. They are inspiring. They quicken the pulse. The Articles' "The said States hereby severally enter into a firm league of friendship with each other" is a dull functional description.

The Revolutionary leaders were not so naïve as to think that amiability was a sound foundation for government. Where money and power are involved, friendship is nice but not enough. There must also be shared conviction, interest, or advantage, backed by power. For a while, the common interest was provided by the need to defeat a common enemy. But with victory over Britain in the Revolutionary War, would there be enough power or common interest to counteract vested State interests, and the differing economies and cultures of the northern, middle, and southern States?

Setting up a new supervening national government to replace the British was not an objective of the Americans as they fought to be free. Little theoretical or political groundwork had been laid in 1776 for the establishment of a general government for all the colonies as they became independent. Montesquieu and others had theorised that republican government was most appropriate in small states, and that for a larger area (as in Switzerland and the Netherlands) a weaker confederation was the appropriate non-monarchical form of government.

Among the most obvious deficiencies of the Articles was that the Confederation had no independent power to tax and enforce payment. It had to invoice each State for its share of the Confederation's expenses and hope that the States would all pay in full. Yet to be able to get anything done a government must have revenue, so that it can pay salaries and buy supplies and services.

There were problems in both political theory and practice with giving a confederate government its own power to tax. It was a maxim of political theory at the time that there could be no "imperium in imperio," or "sovereign state within a sovereign state." Primary power could be delegated, but not split between two governments. It followed that, in theory, a confederate or national government and a state government could not have concurrent powers to collect taxes from the same citizens.

The colonists all knew from English history and from their own recent experience that the power to tax was potentially one of the most oppressive tools in the hands of government. Americans were accustomed to light taxation. The colonies had declined the Albany Plan partly because it would have given a general government a power to tax.

The confederated States were to be known as "The United States of America" (Article I). The title was an exaggeration. There was no union. There was a framework for co-operation: "The Sometimes-Confederated States of America" would have been more accurate—"Sometimes" because the States often chose to not comply with their obligations under the Articles.

Article II provided that: "Each state retains its sovereignty, freedom, and independence, and every power, jurisdiction, and right, which is not by this Confederation expressly delegated to the United States, in Congress assembled." Sovereignty was retained by the States, with limited powers delegated to the "United States in Congress assembled."

An early draft of the Articles by the Dickinson Committee had been far more purposeful. It had provided that the Colonies would unite themselves "into one Body politic" and had made the union binding on both the Colonies and their citizens. The draft had provided, in Article III, that each Colony would keep its powers over its internal affairs *to the extent that they were not inconsistent with the Articles.*[6] This draft would have produced a national government and given it primary (and not merely delegated) power within its areas of responsibility. That was the approach taken in the ultimate Constitution.

The weaker language in the final Articles was intentional. Since the British colonies in America had been established, partial local autonomy had been granted to each colony. Since 1763 all the thinking and energy of the colonists had been directed towards protecting their rights and privileges from a common oppressor, Britain. States were the primary political entities engaged in the fight for freedom—a trans-State Government was perceived as a putative source of new oppression. The objective was to make any such government weak, with just enough power to act as the States' agent in matters requiring their co-operation.

The Articles did not establish any new national state or separate legal entity—the Articles refer to the Government of the Confederation as the "United States in Congress assembled." When Congress duly exercised its delegated powers, it bound the States individually. The States individually remained the relevant legal entities. This is not a pedantic legal detail: it meant that the Confederation could never act without the approval of the States. Which, from the States' perspective, was exactly the intended outcome.

The legal fact that the Articles did not establish a new nation as a new legal entity was reflected in, for example, Article I of the Treaty of Paris of 1783—the treaty pursuant to which the British recognized the independence of the United States. That Article provided that: "His Britannic Majesty acknowledges the said United States, *viz., New Hampshire, Massachusetts Bay, Rhode Island and Providence Plantations, Connecticut, New York, New Jersey, Pennsylvania, Maryland, Virginia, North Carolina, South Carolina and Georgia*, to be free sovereign and independent states . . . [emphasis added]."[7]

The Treaty made it very clear that it was the several States that were the newly independent entities. It did not recognize the United States as a new nation or entity separate from the States. That was a good outcome for the British. Thirteen separate and potentially rivalrous States were less of a challenge to British dominance than a dynamic new nation in the North Atlantic and the Americas.

Executive power was to be exercised by Congress when it was sitting, and by a Committee of the States when it was not. That Committee comprised one delegate from each State. The Committee was to appoint one of its members to preside for not more than one year. This person was the president of the Confederation.

Members of Congress were appointed annually to represent their States. The representatives of each State had one vote between them. A member could not sit for more than three out of any six years. Important issues required the affirmative vote of at least nine States. Citizens played no role in the selection or election of the members of Congress or of the president of the

Confederation: there was no need for direct election because the Confederation was an agent of the States, not a government of the people.

The Confederation was to have exclusive delegated authority to make war or to arrive at peace, and to enter into treaties with other nations. The Confederation was empowered to build and equip a navy, but it had no direct source of revenue to pay for this. For an army, it could decide the number of soldiers that it needed. It then had to requisition the States to supply the troops (in proportion to the number of white inhabitants in each State). Each State was supposed to raise, clothe, and equip its requisitioned troops. Most States failed to meet their quotas. In 1776, for example, Congress voted to raise an army of 75,000 men. Twelve months later, the Army had 28,000 men.[8]

The Articles provided that there was to be free movement of people between the States. The States could continue to regulate and levy taxes on trade between States, as long as the regulation and taxes were not inconsistent with treaties entered into by the United States with foreign nations. The Articles did not establish a free-trade market within the Confederation.

The "United States in Congress assembled" had the power to regulate the mix of metals in coins issued by the Confederation or by any of the States. This power was an attempt to regulate the money supply and to ensure that the value of money was stable. But it was not likely to be effective because coins were a small part of the money supply in Revolutionary America.

Apart from invoicing the States for revenue, the Articles did provide for three possible ways to finance the expenses of the Confederation: printing money, "emitting" bills, and borrowing money.

The power to print money was not exclusive: the States could continue to print their own money. Governments are often tempted to issue paper money to fund their expenses or meet their financial obligations. The problem is that issuing too much money can cause the money to lose value and the sellers of goods and services to raise prices, resulting in price inflation.

The power conferred by the Articles to "emit bills" was a power to issue bonds and debt certificates, a form of funding which had been used by some colonial governments. These instruments often traded as a form of money. Some 13 percent of the total cost to America of the War of Independence was funded by emissions by Congress of bonds and debt certificates.

There was another important prospective source of revenue, although it is not referred to in the Articles: the sale of western lands. The reason that Maryland did not ratify the Articles until March 1, 1781 was that Maryland wanted the States with claims to western lands, based on their original British charters, to cede their claims to Congress.[9] Virginia was the last such State to do so, on January 2, 1781 when it ceded its land west of the Ohio River.

The catastrophe of war did bring economic stimulus, as well as death and destruction. Congress and the States all spent on materials and supplies to sustain the War. Both the French (as allies of the Americans) and the British were spending in America "specie," or gold and silver coinage, for supplies. Amid the carnage and destruction of war, there was strong demand for basic supplies and an inflow of gold and silver coinage to America.

After the Treaty of Paris of 1783, British merchants extended credit to Americans, eager to build or rebuild their presence in the market despite independence. This credit and the spending of the increased supply of gold and silver coinage led to a short post-war boom in imported goods. Then came a period of economic constraint: war spending was over, the States and Congress were servicing and reducing the War debt, and merchants were tighter with their credit.

Now that the States were not part of the British Empire, Britain prohibited American ships from trading with the British Caribbean. The ban was laxly enforced because the islanders needed American supplies at the best available prices.

There was also a financial crisis. Some context is required to understand it.

In the contemporary world, money consists principally of data entries showing deposit accounts at banks. A small proportion of money is in cash or legal tender. In Revolutionary America, the position was more complicated. There were generally no banks. Everyone considered that gold and silver coinage were money. But gold and silver coinage were commonly in short supply, so several paper instruments also performed the function of money as a circulating medium of exchange: paper money issued by the Colonies/States; paper money issued by Congress; but also, various forms of "IOU" certificates issued by both the Colonies/States and Congress. It was as though there were multiple currencies in use in the domestic economy.

The problem with many of these alternative instruments was that they were issued to meet an immediate need of the issuer for funds, and not with a view to maintaining a stable value of money. Their value tended to decline, in some cases dramatically. Each class of instrument had its own value and its own rate of depreciation. So simultaneously some Americans could be experiencing dramatic inflation (as the price of goods and services rose rapidly against the value of the paper money or instruments that they were holding) while other Americans (who held gold and silver coinage, or paper money or instruments whose value was more stable) were not suffering that financial disaster. The better informed and more financially sophisticated Americans were less likely to be caught holding the doubtful money and instruments. The monetary chaos was therefore socially divisive, with the financially unsophisticated feeling that the financially more sophisticated were unfairly getting the better of them. While the soldiers who were risking their lives suffered such devastating hardships, those who were able to benefit from the financial chaos or from war-supply contracts were living well.

The monetary chaos also undermined confidence in the Confederation and rendered it almost impotent at times in carrying on the War. The condition of the Continental Army was often shameful. Its troops were unpaid for long periods. They were poorly fed, sometimes without shelter, shoeless and poorly clothed, and without sufficient munitions. These appalling deficiencies occurred especially after people had lost confidence in Continental dollars, in 1779–81.

Congress did its best to properly fund the War. But as it noted on January 30, 1783: "The inability of Congress to perform the engagements taken with the public creditors will readily appear, when it is considered how defective have been the compliances of the states, in every period of the war."[10]

Congress issued large volumes of Continental dollars, and the British flooded the States with counterfeit dollars to destabilise the wartime economy. The value of Continental dollars declined calamitously: at a hyperinflationary rate of at least 10,000 percent over the six years from 1775 to 1781, when they ceased to be used as money. (That Congress was issuing money from 1775 is a reminder that long before the Articles were formally operative Congress was attempting to co-ordinate and lead the war effort.) "Not worth a Continental" even entered popular usage as a phrase meaning "worthless."

In effect, the depreciation of the Continental dollars was one of the sources of funding of the War. The issue of Continental dollars paid for some 28 percent of those War costs which were met by the Americans.[11] Each holder of a Continental dollar on its journey from issuance to valuelessness indirectly paid for some of the troops' services (or other goods or services) which had initially been bought with that dollar. This contrasted with the American colonial experience of paper money: every currency issuance to fund the Seven Years' War had ultimately been redeemed at face value, although many had traded at discounts to face value before redemption.

A government that issues cash which becomes worthless tends to lose the confidence of its citizens. The most notorious example is that of the Weimar Republic in Germany, where hyperinflation was one of the causes of the failure of that democratic republic and the rise of the National Socialists.

A technique that Congress used to try to halt the collapse in the value of the Continental dollar was to provide that States could use Continental dollars, at a specified depreciated rate, to pay part of the amount for which they had been invoiced by Congress. This was a sound attempt, but was overwhelmed by the scale of the issuance of Continental dollars and the frequent indifference of the States to paying amounts invoiced by Congress.

For many Americans, most of whom were small farmers, the most important "money" was the ledger entries in their local merchants' books. The ledger would be debited when the farmer bought supplies and credited when the farmer sold produce. Such farmers operated in a largely cashless local economy. But they could not use the merchants' ledgers to pay their taxes. How would they get money for that purpose, and which currency or instruments would they use?

The States levied taxes payable in their own currencies, debt certificates, or bonds. This was a way of in effect redeeming the debt certificates or bonds. It also helped to ensure that some forms of money in circulation in the State had value. Sometimes taxes were assessed on a basis which reflected the market depreciation of the different forms of money. The depreciation of State currencies was much less dramatic than that of the Continental dollar. Money became directly politicised because the States' decisions about what currency or instruments they would accept (and at what rate) for the payment of taxes were so important to their individual citizens.

The States assumed ultimate responsibility for about two-fifths of wartime expenditure.[12]

The French contributed a significant amount to the war effort through gifts of supplies, loans, and, at French cost, deploying land and naval forces that participated in the War. These direct costs amounted to perhaps a quarter of the total costs of the Americans and the French.[13] For the French King (Louis XVI), the American war was a war against his perennial enemy, the British, with the potential for a new American nation to emerge as a French ally or client state. Ironically, in a reminder of the political importance of sound public finance, the debt assumed by the French King in fighting this war worsened the already fragile French national finances and contributed to the heavy taxation in France which was an important cause of the French Revolution.

With the decisive American and French victory over the British at Yorktown in October 1781, Dutch investors had sufficient confidence in the prospects of the United States to lend $2.8 million at 5 percent per annum. Amsterdam was the principal capital market of the day outside Britain. Notwithstanding the chaos of American domestic monetary value, and the fact that the Confederation was only an agent of the States, the Dutch trusted the Americans to meet their obligations to pay interest and to repay the principal on this loan. There was good reason for that, despite the deficiencies in the Articles. The Americans had honoured all their obligations arising from the Seven Years' War.

The financial problems during the War of Independence arose from the absence of a taxation power in the Government of the Confederation, and from emissions of cash and debt instruments that depreciated quickly in the domestic market. The holders of that cash and those instruments suffered: but the Americans knew that their standing in international markets was important to their ability to attract capital, and they found ways to meet their foreign commitments. The magnitude of the foreign loans to be serviced was only 6 percent of the total American costs of funding the War.[14]

It was widely recognized in America in the early 1780s that the powers conferred under the Articles were too limited. Many of those who wanted a national and not merely a federal government to address the deficiency had been soldiers during the War. They had first-hand experience of the near collapse of the Continental Army because of a lack of money and resources. The victory at Yorktown weakened the argument of the former-soldier nationalists, that more power in a federal or national Government was required to deliver military capability. Contrary to their predictions, the War had been won (with substantial French help) despite the Confederation's impotence. But none of the troops would ever forget the privations that they had suffered, and that from early 1781 they had not even been paid in depreciating Continentals. They had served and risked everything on a promise of future payment. In 1783 they eventually received interest-bearing debt certificates.

Another group who generally had a "Continentalist" outlook, wanting a stronger federal government, were merchants and traders. They were strong especially in Philadelphia and New York. They wanted a reliable national currency and a single system of taxation and regulation for trade.

Southern plantation owners were sceptical, fearing that the merchant interests would misuse their power in a federal government if the Southern States lost their power to tax and regulate trade. But the South did want the new nation to be able to defend itself and to open western lands between the Appalachians and the Mississippi. In those lands there were conflicts with Native Americans. Farmers in the western lands would get their produce to market via the Mississippi. As some of those lands were still occupied by the British, and the Spanish were trying to exclude American shipping from the Mississippi, Southerners needed an internationally credible government with the ability to act on the ground.

A fourth group with a "Continentalist" outlook were younger members of Congress, who had "become politically active during the revolutionary struggle . . . [and whose] vision had been shaped by their focus on attaining national goals: American independence, American victory, and the establishment of a powerful republican nation."[15]

Alexander Hamilton was not a scion of a family with vested interests in the economic, governance or social arrangements in any State. He had arrived in America in 1772 as a brilliant orphan of fifteen[16] from St Croix, the Caribbean place of his birth (then in the British Empire, now in the US Virgin

Islands). He served in the Continental Army from 1776 to 1781. He joined General George Washington,[17] the Commander in Chief of the American forces, as an aide-de-camp in 1777. Aged 24, Hamilton had also commanded an infantry brigade in the final assault at Yorktown, where he showed firmness and bravery under fire.

His experience of America in his formative years was therefore strongly Continentalist. He had served with the leader of the only substantial Continental institution, the Army. He saw at first hand both the debilitating effect on the Army's capability and the suffering of its soldiers, caused by Congress' inability to command sufficient funds and to raise more troops. He reached the conclusion that America needed a more powerful national Government. Hamilton had the intelligence and confidence to argue his case articulately and publicly. In 1781 and 1782, he wrote six short articles which were published under the title "The Continentalist," arguing in support of proposals to amend the Articles to confer more powers on the federal Government: ". . . in [Congress'] present form, it is unequal, either to a vigorous prosecution of the war, or to the preservation of the union in peace . . ."[18]

Hamilton would later play a leading role in the campaign for a new Constitution. For present purposes, what is striking is that his views were well formed already in 1781 and that the first "The Continentalist" article appeared only months after the inadequate Articles of Confederation legally came into effect.

In August 1780, a convention had been held in Boston, with representatives of Massachusetts, Connecticut and New Hampshire attending to consider what could be done about the perilous state of both the Army and the Confederation's finances. New York approved of its resolutions and, along with Rhode Island, agreed to send representatives to a further convention at Hartford.

Eleven of the resolutions of the Boston convention were entreaties to the States to take action to address immediate problems: financial deficiencies, and the raising of troops and supplies for the Army. Resolution twelve addressed the deficiencies in the Articles, which, in August 1780, had not yet come into formal effect: " . . . [this Convention] conceive[s] it to be essential to our final Safety, to the establishment of public Credit, and to put a speedy and happy Issue to the present calamitous War, *that the Union of these States be fixed in a more Solid and permanent Manner, that the Powers of Congress be more clearly ascertained and defined* [emphasis added]."[19]

This resolution also proposed that executive power be vested in one supreme head—a proposal to rectify the weakness of the executive function under the Articles. Until the terms of the Articles could be formally amended, the resolution proposed that the States delegate extra powers to their representatives in Congress. The need was urgent. There was no time to wait for the formal process required to amend the Articles.

When it came to judicial power, the delegated powers of the Confederation (set out in clause IX of the Articles of Confederation) were limited to appointing courts: ". . . for the trial of piracies and felonies committed on the high seas and . . . for receiving and determining finally appeals in all cases of captures [on the high seas]" and to being "the last resort on appeal in all disputes and differences . . . between two or more States concerning boundary, jurisdiction or any other causes whatever . . ."

What could the Confederation do if a State ignored one of the Confederation's invoices or requisitions? The Articles were silent on this question. If Congress authorised the commencement of legal proceedings, the "United States in Congress assembled" could presumably sue in the delinquent State's Courts and hope for both a fair judgment and effective enforcement. But to take such action would require the support of the representatives of at least nine States. Congress never attempted to use State Courts to enforce compliance with its requisitions, so the Courts played no role in enforcing the Articles against the States.

The Hartford convention was held in November 1780 and was attended by representatives of the four New England States and of New York. It also passed resolutions imploring the States to comply with Congress's requisitions. It did not resolve that the Articles be amended but did, alarmingly, resolve that the Army should be able to use force against the States: ". . . that the Commander in Chief of the Army of the United States be Authorized and Impowered to take such Measures as he may deem proper . . . to induce the several States to a punctual Compliance with the Requisitions which have been or may be made by Congress for Supplies for the Years 1780 and 1781."[20] The Articles contained no mechanism to peacefully enforce payment of Congress's invoices or compliance with its requisitions. In the absence of a Court of law with the jurisdiction and enforcement capability to compel non-complying States, violence would have to be used.

In March 1781, a committee of Congress (whose members included James Madison, who was to play a major role in shaping the final Constitution) recommended to Congress an amendment to the Articles, along the lines of the recommendation of the Hartford Convention, to give Congress coercive power to use force against delinquent States: ". . . the said United States in Congress assembled [would be] fully authorised to employ the force of the United States as well by sea as by land to compel . . . such State or States to fulfill their federal engagements . . . untill [sic] full compensation or compliance be obtained with respect to all Requisitions . . ."[21]

Members of Congress were all representatives of the States. Congress did not accept the Committee's recommendation. It is astonishing that the Committee presumably believed that the proposal had some chance of being approved by Congress.

In February 1781 Congress passed a resolution requesting power to levy a 5 percent import duty on most goods, for the purpose of servicing its debts. This proposal gained some momentum until victory at Yorktown saw support evaporate for helping Congress deal with its financial problems.

Congress again sought power to impose an import duty in 1783 after representatives of the Army presented a petition for the benefits that were due to the troops. This proposal gained the support of all the States—except New York, which in 1785 rejected it. There was no subsequent attempt to amend the Articles to give Congress its own source of revenue.

Attempts to give Congress the sole power to regulate trade also failed. After the War, anti-British sentiment and the British prohibition on American ships trading with the British Caribbean, plus a desire to assist the development of American shipping, led to most States adopting measures which favoured American over British shipping and products. In 1783, Maryland authorised its delegates in Congress to support an amendment to the Articles which would give Congress power to prohibit imports and exports of foreign goods in vessels that were not American. Virginia favoured giving Congress the power to impose a ban on imports from the British Caribbean in British vessels.

In April 1784, Congress asked the States to grant it additional powers to regulate trade with foreign States. The request was for a delegation of power for fifteen years, not for an amendment to the Articles. The request did not extend to any power over interstate trade. The April request had not been granted by the States when, in late 1784, Congress turned again to the issue of its power to regulate trade by appointing a committee chaired by James Monroe (later the fifth President of the United States).

While the regulation of trade remained with the States, not only was regulation not uniform: it was susceptible to local political influence. Merchants found that they were losing out to local manufacturers. Manufacturing had been boosted during the War by the restrictions on Atlantic trade and the need for materials. Now manufacturers sought, and sometimes got, tariffs on imported goods, to give themselves a competitive advantage in the American market. This was contrary to the interests of merchants and shippers.

The Monroe Committee reported in March 1785, recommending that the Articles be amended to give Congress almost exclusive power to regulate both international and interstate trade. This power should include the power to levy imposts on traded goods, although the revenues raised would belong to the States, not to the Government of the Confederation. The States could, however, prohibit the import or export of any goods. This power would presumably encompass the slave trade.

In its reasons, the Committee emphasized the difficulty of concluding trade agreements with other nations under the arrangements in the Articles. It was true that the Articles forbade imposts or duties which were inconsistent with trade treaties. But other nations "apprehend it will be difficult for thirteen different Legislatures acting separately and distinctly to agree in the same interpretation of a treaty, to take the same measures, for carrying it into effect . . ."[22]

The Committee's recommendations were not adopted by Congress.

The task of reforming the Confederation was hopeless. None of its failures in raising and supplying military forces, its fatal lack of revenue, or its impotence in regulating trade, could be fixed.

By failing to adapt the Confederation model, the defenders of the status quo led nationalists, or "Continentalists," to pursue a high-risk campaign for an entirely new system. The Continentalists included men of brilliance, whose ideas and tactics were shaped and refined during the agonising frustrations of the Confederation period. Their vision and skill led to a new foundation for the American nation.

NOTES

1. As noted in chapter 6, the War began with the battles of Lexington and Concord in April 1775. The decisive American victory was at Yorktown in October 1781, but the Treaty of Paris was not signed until September 1783.

2. "Albany Plan of Union, 1754." The Avalon Project, Yale Law School. Accessed September 2018 to July 2020. https://avalon.law.yale.edu/18th_century/albany.asp.

3. "Articles of Confederation as presented to Congress" in the *Journals of the Continental Congress*, July 12, 1777, Volume 5 page 546. Library of Congress 1906. Accessed January 2019. https://memory.loc.gov/cgi-bin/ampage?collId=lljc&fileName=005/lljc005.db&recNum=130.

4. "Articles of Confederation." The Avalon Project, Yale Law School. Accessed October 2018 to July 2020. https://avalon.law.yale.edu/18th_century/artconf.asp.

5. Many people have heard of the Confederacy of the Civil War period, but not of the Confederation. The Confederacy did not exist until 1861 and was formed by States that purported to secede from the United States.

6. ("Articles of Confederation as presented to Congress.")

7. ("Treaty of Paris, 1763")

8. Ferling, John E. 2003. *A Leap in the Dark: The Struggle to Create the American Republic*. Oxford University Press, 217.

9. Virginia's 1609 Charter, for example, granted it land extending west to the Pacific Ocean (". . . and all that Space and Circuit of Land, lying from the Sea Coast of the Precinct aforesaid, up into the Land throughout from Sea to Sea, West and Northwest . . ."). Maryland was not acting for the benefit of Congress: it wanted to clear obstacles to the claims of Marylanders who had bought western land from Native Americans.

10. *Journals of the Continental Congress*. January 30, 1783, Volume 24. Library of Congress 1922, HathiTrust Digital Library, page 102. Accessed April 2019. https://babel.hathitrust.org/cgi/pt?id=msu.31293020542753&view=1up&seq=116.

11. Perkins, Edward J. 1994. *American Public Finance and Financial Services 1700-1815*. Ohio State University Press, Table 5.4.

12. (Perkins 1994), 100.

13. (Perkins 1994), 104.

14. (Perkins 1994), 104.

15. (Ferling 2003), 235

16. It is not certain whether the year of his birth was 1755 or 1757.

17. In 1976 Washington was posthumously promoted to the rank of "General of the Armies of the United States." In 1775 his commission appointed him as "General and Commander in Chief of the army of the United Colonies."

18. Hamilton, Alexander. 1781. "The Continentalist. No. 1." National Archives. Accessed June 2019. https://founders.archives.gov/documents/Hamilton/01-02-02-1179.

19. *Proceedings of a Convention of Delegates . . . Held at Boston August 3–9, 1780*. J. Munsell,1867, page 50. Accessed July 2019. https://babel.hathitrust.org/cgi/pt?id=loc.ark:/13960/t5db8pn1n&view=1up&seq=58.

20. Charles J. Hoadly ed., *The Public Records of the State of Connecticut* Hartford, Case, Lockwood & Brainard Co. 1894, 1895, 1922 at 571, cited in Natleson, Robert G. 2013. "Founding-Era Conventions and the meaning of The Constitution's 'Convention for proposing Amendments.'" *Florida Law Review* 65 (May 2013 Number 3): 644.

21. Madison, James. "Proposed Amendment of Articles of Confederation," [12 March] 1781. National Archives. Accessed August 2019. https://founders.archives.gov/documents/Madison/01-03-02-0007.

22. *Journals of the Continental Congress*. March 28, 1785, Volume 28, page 202. Library of Congress 1933, HathiTrust Digital Library. Accessed August 2019. https://babel.hathitrust.org/cgi/pt?id=hvd.32044116229097&view=1up&seq=218&q1=apprehend%20AND%20it%20AND%20will.

Chapter Eight

The Revolution is Secured

The Constitution is Born

The Constitution did not just fix the flaws in the Articles of Confederation. It introduced a different form of government, a federal but also a national government, with a stronger executive and judiciary: a government which would be difficult for any one political faction or economic interest to dominate.

There was enough strength in the general government established by the Constitution to enable the increase of the Union from thirteen to fifty States—a weak confederated structure could not have functioned with such massive expansion. But the States remained powerful enough to allow substantial differences in the government of the different economic and cultural regions of the nation.

Under its Constitution, the United States has risen from a free, prosperous, and rapidly developing group of thirteen former British colonies to be the most powerful nation in the world—a nation that also leads in innovation, individual rights, freedom, and prosperity; and that has more than once played a leading role in saving much of the world from enslavement and tyranny. All this is not solely down to the Constitution. But by setting out and protecting a new and functional system of government built on individual liberty, the common law, the rule of law, representative government, and a separation and balance of powers, the Constitution has been a key enabler.

The new Constitution was not planned or sought by Congress. It was conceived by a subversive group of nationalist leaders, acting beyond the scope of their authority.

Congress resolved on February 21, 1787 that:

> ... on the second Monday in May next a Convention of delegates ... appointed by the several States be held in Philadelphia for the sole and express purpose of *revising the Articles of Confederation and reporting to Congress and the*

several [State] legislatures such alterations and provisions therein [emphasis added] as shall when agreed to in Congress and confirmed by the States render the Constitution adequate to the exigencies of Government and the preservation of the Union.[1]

Yet what the Convention was to report to Congress and the State legislatures was not revisions and alterations. The Convention drafted and recommended an entirely new Constitution which would establish a fundamentally new system of government.

The catalyst for Congress' resolution seeking revisions to the Articles was a report on the proceedings of the Annapolis Convention. The Commissioners who attended in Annapolis (representing Virginia, Delaware, Pennsylvania, New Jersey, and New York) in September 1786 found themselves of like mind and reported to their State legislatures and to Congress that:

- to enable a uniform system of trade may require adjustment to aspects of the federal system beyond those that expressly related to trade;
- there may be numerous defects in the current system of federal government which "merit a deliberate and candid discussion . . . [and that a Convention of Deputies should be convened] for the special and sole purpose of entering into [an investigation of these defects], and digesting a plan for supplying such defects as may be discovered to exist"; and
- the proposed convention should also *"devise such further provisions as shall appear to them necessary to render the constitution of the Federal Government adequate to the exigencies of the Union* [emphasis added]."[2]

Earlier in their report the Annapolis Commissioners had noted that the object of their meeting was to consider the provisions of the Articles that related to "the Trade and Commerce of the United States" but they "did not conceive it advisable to proceed on the business of their mission, under the Circumstance of so partial and defective a representation." So, a poorly attended meeting at Annapolis which had been convened to consider the allocation of trade powers under the Confederation chose to promote a general review of the system of government established by the Articles. The recommendations of this meeting, which was not quorate and had acted beyond the scope of its authority, became the foundation of Congress' resolution to convene the Constitutional Convention in Philadelphia. That Convention drafted the final Constitution.

Seven of the twelve Commissioners later attended the Philadelphia Convention, including: from New York, Alexander Hamilton; from Delaware, John Dickinson, and Richard Bassett; and from Virginia, Edmund Randolph, and James Madison (who would be the primary author of "the Virginia Plan," which did much to shape the deliberations in Pennsylvania).

Not only did the Annapolis meeting successfully call for the Philadelphia Convention and provide some of the leading nationalist proponents there: Annapolis helped the nationalists to mobilize and prepare for the final Convention. Fifty-five delegates attended in Philadelphia to determine what defects of the Confederation needed to be fixed and to recommend a solution. Those without a plan and without organization were not going to prevail in so large a group with such an expansive task. After Annapolis, the nationalists worked to capture the initiative and to prevail in Philadelphia. They succeeded.

The nationalists got lucky, too. Shays' Rebellion broke out in early 1787. The economy had recovered from postwar inflation and adjustment. Massachusetts had been retiring its war debt aggressively, funded by greatly increased taxes from some two percent of aggregate State income to between eight to eleven percent. The enormous tax increases both reduced demand for farmers' products and increased farmers' costs. Many farmers defaulted on their tax and other debts. Farms and crops were seized. The crisis was most acute in the west of the State. When Shays and some 2,000 armed civilians marched on the federal arsenal at Springfield in January 1787, the State Government sent in troops to suppress the rebellion.[3]

Shays' Rebellion had little to do with Congress or the Confederation. It was caused by a very aggressive policy for the elimination of the Massachusetts' State debt. But the fact that the Rebellion occurred fomented anxiety about the state of government in the Confederation. That anxiety helped the nationalists.

The nationalists were keen that George Washington attend the Philadelphia Convention. His prestige as a national leader was immense. Washington believed that the federal Government needed more powers: how could he not, after watching the privations of his army during the War? Before agreeing to attend, he waited for Congress to endorse the plan for the Convention, and to be confident that at least a quorum of States was likely to be represented. He did attend and was elected President of the Convention.

THE PHILADELPHIA CONVENTION

The Philadelphia Convention began on May 25, 1787. Most of the delegates were men of property and position. All States were represented except Rhode Island, which had chosen not to send delegates. The Convention took place in the Pennsylvania State House, where Congress had declared independence in 1776. The venue must have impressed upon the delegates the profound, paramount importance of their task.

Governor Randolph of Virginia spoke first and recommended the following method. The Convention should inquire into:

- the powers and capacity which a federal Government ought to possess;
- the defects of the Confederation;
- the danger of the situation of the Confederation; and
- the remedy.

He traversed the shortcomings of government under the Articles of Confederation, including in mobilizing and funding military forces, in not having a secure source of revenue, in being dependent on the States, and in having no mechanism for checking quarrels between States. He did not mention the regulation of trade.

Randolph suggested that the Articles could not deliver their own objects of "[securing the States'] common defense, the security of their liberties, and their mutual and general welfare . . ." (Article III). This was a shrewd reference. It implied that any proposal to advance the *purposes* of the Articles was within the scope of the Convention's mandate from Congress.

Randolph also said: "Our chief danger arises from the democratic parts of our constitutions. It is a maxim which I hold incontrovertible, that the powers of government exercised by the people swallows [sic] up the other branches. None of the constitutions have provided sufficient checks against the democracy."[4]

"Democratic" and "democracy" in this context meant the unchecked power of the majority of voters (which I touched on in chapter 6). Randolph was not suggesting that members of the legislature should not be elected. He was referring to one of the inherent risks of democracy: that the majority might oppress the minority. If this is done through specific laws, it denies fairness and justice to the minority. If it is done through constraining or reducing the political rights of the minority, it destroys the system itself. Randolph was probably also referring to the risk that overly powerful legislatures impeded the effectiveness of the executive branch of government ("that the powers of government exercised by the people swallows [sic] up the other *branches*").

The questions were how a government elected by a majority of the eligible free white male population could be checked from oppressing other citizens, and how the powers of the different branches of government should be allocated and checked. Madison considered that the diversity of interests and opinions that would subsist in such a large country as the United States, with a wide range of economic and sectional interests, coupled with checks and balances in the structure of the government, could achieve this with the right design. As recorded in his own notes, on June 6 Madison made a long contribution to the discussion on the method of election of members of the House, which contained references to political theory and history, and included:

> The only remedy is to enlarge the sphere, & thereby divide the community into so great a number of interests & parties, that in the [first] place a majority will not be likely . . . to have a common interest separate from that of the whole or of the minority; and in the [second] place, that in case they [should] have such an interest, they may not be apt to unite in the pursuit of it. It was incumbent on us then to try this remedy, and with that view *to frame a republican system on such a scale & in such a form as will controul all the evils [which] have been experienced* [emphasis added].[5]

The Convention did find ways to introduce safeguards "against the democracy," or what is often called "the tyranny of the majority." Through its two houses of Congress, its elected executive (partly constrained by Congress), and its judiciary, the new Constitution was to distribute power more widely than the State Constitutions or the Articles of Confederation had done. There was to be a significant separation of powers, and checks on those powers, making it difficult to effect impetuous and radical majoritarian change in law or government.

Unlike Alexander Hamilton, James Madison had not become a nationalist as a result of spending his earliest adult years in the Continental Army. He came from an influential and wealthy family in Virginia. Four years after leaving Princeton, he was elected to the Virginian State assembly. He soon moved to the Council of State, which advised the Governor of Virginia. He was elected to Congress in 1780, at the age of thirty.

Initially he supported the lack of powers in the Articles, happy to see Virginia maintain its power and importance as the pre-eminent State. But the success of the British in the War with their Southern strategy in 1779–81, and the inability of the United States to resolve access to the Mississippi with Spain in 1786, helped to convince him of the need for a more potent national government. Madison set himself the task of devising a constitutional system which would vest sufficient power in a federal or a national government to enable it to function effectively, but to restrain the power of its different organs, and to restrain any "levelling spirit" among the elected representatives.[6]

He was the primary author of the Virginia Plan, which was introduced to the Convention by Governor Randolph on May 29, 1787, and proposed that:

- the Articles ought to confer sufficient powers to enable the federal government to accomplish the objects of the Articles, being common defense, security of liberty and general welfare;
- representation in Congress should be proportionate to revenue contributed, or to the number of free inhabitants;
- Congress should have two houses: members of the first house should be directly elected by eligible citizens, and members of the second house should be nominated by the State legislatures and elected by the members of the first house;
- Congress and the State legislatures should have distinct powers to legislate;
- Congress should be able to negative State legislation "contravening in the opinion of the National Legislature the articles of Union";
- the Union should be able to use force against a recalcitrant State;
- there should be a President, chosen by Congress for a seven-year term;
- there should be a National Judiciary with jurisdiction extending to tax enforcement and interstate disputes;
- there should be a Council of Revision, composed of the Executive and members of the National Judiciary with the power to examine and veto Congress' legislation, which veto could be overridden by Congress (remember the Council of Revision in the New York State Constitution of 1777?);
- executives and judges of the States should be bound by oath to support the amended Articles; and
- the amendments to the Articles should be put to a directly elected assembly or assemblies "to consider and decide thereon . . ."[7]

A plan was also presented on May 29, by Charles Pinkney of South Carolina. Pinkney's plan provided, in effect, that the Government should be both a federal and national government. The Government should have exclusive power with respect to revenue imposts and trade. State laws would not be effective until approved by Congress. There should be an Executive branch. The States should retain all powers not expressly granted to the federal Government.

Madison acquired great authority over the story of what happened at the Convention, because he kept the most comprehensive notes of its proceedings and because later in life he wrote extensively about the events at Philadelphia. A distinguished historian of the Convention has observed that: " . . . Pinkney's claims to making an important, if not *the* most important, contribution to the Convention are far stronger than Madison was willing to admit. . . . [Other historians have concluded that Pinkney's] proposals to the Convention did constitute 'a noteworthy contribution to the Constitution.'"[8]

Also, on May 29, the Convention decided that details of its deliberations should be kept secret: "That nothing spoken in the House be printed, or otherwise published or communicated without leave." The delegates adhered to this rule of secrecy, and that was important in enabling them to reach compromises without endless interference from opinionated citizens in their respective States.

The Convention made rapid progress on key features of the new system. On May 30, it agreed that there should be a national Government consisting of a supreme legislature, executive and judiciary.

In his notes on proceedings on May 30, Madison recorded Colonel George Mason (Virginia) as saying that the new government would need the power to enforce its laws against individuals, and not just against States. That was a fundamental principle. It was adopted. It imposed on individual citizens obligations to the new government and was one of the features that gave the new government a national, and not just a confederated, character. It meant that enforcement of the laws of the new government could operate in a normal way, with orders and sanctions being sought against recalcitrant individuals and not against States. (States might in some circumstances have both the inclination and the means to ignore or resist national laws.)

The next day, Madison said that the more he reflected on that part of the Virginia Plan which provided that the Union should be able to use force against a non-complying State, the more he doubted its practicality, justice, and efficacy, and realized that it would look like a declaration of war. His depth of frustration with the Articles must have been profound to have ever contemplated the use of the Army against States as a constitutional enforcement mechanism. That mechanism would have led to *constitutionally sanctioned* and recurrent civil war.

On May 31, the Convention agreed that Congress should have two houses; that legislation should be able to be initiated by either house; and that Congress' legislative power should extend to areas expressly granted to it, areas where the States were not competent, and areas where State legislation would interrupt the harmony of the United States.

All agreed that the Confederation was defective, that a stronger general government was required, and that the States should continue. This common ground was vital. The Confederation system had been given enough time for its defects to be overwhelming and incontrovertible. Had the Convention met a year or two earlier, some delegates might still have hoped that it could be saved. Had it occurred much later, the Confederation may have split or dissolved and any attempt to form a new union may have faced more entrenched localism. As the Convention moved on to more challenging issues, the delegates' awareness that the Confederation was fatally flawed compelled them to compromise and to work to design a better system.

It is striking that the discussions which framed the debates in the Convention did not focus on virtuous citizenry, the strand of republican political philosophy that had been prominent up to Independence and, as noted in chapter 6, especially in Article 15 of Virginia's Declaration of Rights. Perhaps it was the context. The States had demonstrated that they did not always honor their commitments, and the Convention was seeking a workable alternative to the failed system established by the Articles. The approach taken by the Convention was more mechanistic. There was no assumption that in matters of government people would always be virtuous. The new machinery of government needed to allow for people's failings as well as their virtues.

The tone and quality of the Convention debates are striking. The fact that the proceedings were secret helped. Different opinions were expressed clearly, and well argued. The discussion was generally civil. Responses suggest that delegates were listening to other delegates. There were compromises and changes of mind after hearing other opinions. At times, the debates were strained, but they were never vituperative or abusive. Some of this constructive and reasonable tone may be attributable to how Madison chose to record proceedings in his notes.

The allocation of powers between the proposed new federal government and the States was not addressed early in the debates. The Virginia Plan addressed the extent of the powers of the proposed new government by stating two principles, not by attempting to specifically articulate and allocate powers:

- "that the Articles of Confederation ought to be so corrected and enlarged as to accomplish the objects proposed by their institution; namely, 'common defence, security of liberty and general welfare.'"; and
- "that the National Legislature ought to be impowered to enjoy the Legislative Rights vested in Congress by the Confederation and moreover to legislate in all cases to which the separate States are incompetent, or in which the harmony of the United States may be interrupted by the exercise of individual Legislation."

On May 30, John Dickinson (Delaware) identified the importance of focusing on the scope of powers, as well as the machinery of the new government. He said that the Convention should determine what legislative powers should be vested in Congress, what powers in the judiciary, and what powers in the executive. William Paterson's (New Jersey) plan of June 15 set out several of the key powers that the federal government should have (including specific revenue powers, and powers over interstate and international trade).

On July 16 it was resolved unanimously "That the National Legislature ought to possess the Legislative Rights vested in Congress by the Confederation."[9]

Detailed discussion about federal powers mainly occurred in August, when the Convention was considering a draft of the proposed Constitution. The final Constitution did specify (in Article I, Section 8) the scope of Congress' legislative power, and it is no surprise considering the history of the War and the Confederation that the list of powers included the power to tax; to declare war and raise and maintain military forces; to borrow money; to regulate trade with foreign nations, among the States, and with Native American Nations; and to coin money and fix its value. The final power was: "To make all Laws which shall be necessary and proper" for implementing the express powers.

To further delineate the boundary between Federal and State powers, sections 9 and 10 of Article 1 prohibited the States from engaging in certain activities. Some prohibitions sought to protect individual rights (for example, a State could not suspend habeas corpus), several were to prohibit State restrictions on trade, some prohibited State currencies, and others prohibited the States from entering treaties with foreign states. Sections 9 and 10 also imposed restrictions on the federal government, including that it could only spend money pursuant to appropriations approved by Congress and could not grant titles of nobility.

Which were the hardest issues for the Convention to resolve? They included:

• the extent to which States should be represented (if at all) in Congress;
• the continuation of the slave trade; and
• the mode of election and powers of the President.

The contentiousness of the first and second of these issues is reflected in Article V of the Constitution, which prohibited any amendment which would deny (without consent) any State equal representation in the Senate or would authorize the abolition of the slave trade before 1808.

Some of the hard issues came up in the earliest days of the Convention but were deferred after discussion. The Convention wisely identified issues on which agreement could be quickly reached, giving its work real momentum.

On the question of who should elect or appoint the members of the first house of Congress, for example, Mr. Pinkney (South Carolina) moved that they should be appointed by the States, arguing that "the people were less fit judges in such a case, and that the [States] would be less likely to promote the adoption of the new Government, if they were to be excluded from all share in it."[10]

Mr. Gerry[11] (Massachusetts) suggested a variant, noting that in Massachusetts direct election had resulted in "the worst men get[ting] into the legislature. Several members of that body had lately been convicted of infamous crimes."[12] He proposed that the people should nominate candidates chosen from several districts, and the State legislature should choose from those candidates. Mr Wilson (Pennsylvania) argued for direct election by the people, as the source of all authority – he considered that large electorates would reduce the risk of bad men intriguing themselves into office. Mr Sherman (Connecticut) argued that to preserve harmony between the States and the national government, the elections to the national legislature should be made by the States. Colonel Mason (Virginia) argued that if the national government were to operate on individuals, they should elect the members of the first house. Madison was also for direct elections by the people.

There were other contributions to the debate. The proposal that members of the first house of Congress should be appointed by the States was defeated.

The Virginia Plan had proposed that members of the second house be elected by the members of the first. Smaller States were thus exposed to a risk of two types of dilution of power. The first was a consequence of vesting substantive powers in the new national government, diminishing the powers of every State. The second was in diluting the small States' representation in Congress according to population.

The Constitution would come into effect when it was ratified by nine of the thirteen States, so the support of smaller States was essential. (The data in Appendix 2 show a huge spread of population sizes between the States, with Virginia's total population being more than ten times that of each of Delaware and Rhode Island.)

William Paterson's "New Jersey Plan" provided, in effect, that Congress should have only one house, in which the States would be equally represented, as under the Articles of Confederation. This was a bombshell. It would mean the retention of a confederated structure of government, with no national element and no ability to enforce its laws directly against individuals. It would protect the smaller and middling States at the cost of continuing with a failed system. Until what? The breaking up of the Confederation into rival nations or federations? Increased European influence on a divided continent with no effective co-ordination between its puny States?

On June 18, Alexander Hamilton countered with a plan that had no element of State representation, and under which senators and the President (or "Governor") would serve from election until death, resignation, or removal (by impeachment). It had no federal elements, and the appointment of important office holders for life was too aristocratic, or even monarchical, for the Convention.

On July 2, a vote was taken, and the delegates were deadlocked on the question of whether the States should each have equal representation in the second house of Congress. General Pinkney (South Carolina) proposed that a committee consisting of a member from each State should be appointed to devise and report some compromise. Some delegates considered compromise impossible. Delegates threatened to leave the Convention if their position did not prevail. After further debate, the Convention referred the problem to a committee. The Convention adjourned until it could receive the Committee's report. The future of the United States was in the balance.

On July 5, the Committee reported its recommendations: "1. That in the 1st. branch of the Legislature each of the States now in the Union shall be allowed 1 member for every 40,000 inhabitants . . . that each State not containing that number shall be allowed 1 member . . . 2. That in the 2d. branch each State shall have an equal vote."[13]

On July 16, the Convention accepted the compromise (40,000 inhabitants was later reduced to 30,000). On July 23 it resolved that each State should be represented by two senators. The Great Compromise, as it is sometimes called, is in similar terms to a proposal of Roger Sherman's (Connecticut) way back on June 11. It is sometimes called "the Connecticut Plan." Sherman's foresight and judgement were remarkable—it took the Convention five weeks of testing debate to see that he had already found the way to balance popular and State representation in the new Congress.

The final Constitution provided that the House of Representatives would "be composed of Members chosen every second Year by the People of the several States" (Article I Section 2) and the Senate would be "composed of two Senators from each State, chosen by the legislature thereof" (Article I Section 3). In 1913, the Seventeenth Amendment provided that Senators would be chosen by the people of each State, so the Senate morphed from being a "States' House" to a "House of the people of each State."

Another of the hardest issues was, of course, how to deal with slavery. Pennsylvania, New Hampshire, and Rhode Island had already begun its gradual abolition. Slavery was unconstitutional in Massachusetts, on the basis that it was inconsistent with that State's Declaration of Rights (which included in Article I that: "All men are born free and equal, and have certain natural, essential, and unalienable rights; among which may be reckoned the right of enjoying and defending their lives and liberties . . .").[14]

It was not formally proposed at the Convention that the federal government should have the power to abolish slavery. Debates focused on whether the federal government should use its proposed power over international trade to prohibit the importation of slaves; whether the importation of slaves should be subject to a federal trade impost; and whether slaves should be counted as part of the population when determining representation in the first house of Congress.

Some delegates considered slavery immoral and wanted the national government to end it entirely. Most delegates seem to have considered slavery at least morally undesirable. (The word "slavery" does not appear in the Constitution. Slavery is referred to by euphemisms.) But some States considered it economically essential. In Maryland, Delaware and Virginia, opinions were mixed, and included strong anti-slavery opinions.

Most States had abolished the importation of slaves—only North Carolina, South Carolina and Georgia still permitted it. Georgia and South Carolina were still developing the potential of their agriculture and plantations (and their rice fields may have caused higher slave mortality rates than other forms of agriculture[15]), and insisted that they needed time to build up their slave populations by importation. Their delegates repeatedly asserted that if they were thwarted in this need, their States would not join the Union. Other States that used slaves in agriculture had sufficient slave populations (remembering that the children of slaves were themselves slaves) and did not consider that they needed to import slaves.[16]

The position of the southernmost States was put starkly in realpolitikal terms by Mr. Rutledge (South Carolina) on August 21:

> Religion & humanity had nothing to do with this question. Interest alone is the governing principle with nations. The true question at present is whether the Southn. States shall or shall not be parties to the Union. If the Northern States consult their interest, they will not oppose the increase of Slaves which will increase the commodities of which they will become the carriers.[17]

In contrast, Colonel Mason a slaveowner from Virginia, objected to slavery on social and moral grounds: ". . . Slavery discourages arts & manufactures. The poor despise labor when performed by slaves. . . . They produce the most pernicious effect on manners. Every master of slaves is born a petty tyrant. They bring the judgment of heaven on a Country."[18]

The compromises reached on the issues of whether the federal government should use its power to prohibit the importation of slaves and whether the importation of slaves should be subject to a federal trade impost were set out in Article I Section 9 of the Constitution, which prohibited the national government from banning the importation of slaves before 1808 and allowed that, in the meantime, importation could be taxed at up to ten dollars per slave.

When it came to fixing revenue obligations, it was in the South's interests to minimise the number of slaves counted. When it came to determining the South's representation in the House of Representatives, it was in the South's interests to maximize the number of slaves counted. The debate over whether slaves should be counted ended up settling on the compromise that had been reached in another context in 1783.

Article VIII of the Articles of Confederation provided that States should fund the Confederation in proportion to the relative value of all land in each State. This was found to be manipulable and unworkable, and on April 18, 1783 Congress had proposed an amendment to the Articles which would use population size as the basis for fixing the relative financial contributions of the States to the Confederation. This gave rise to the question of whether to count slaves in the population. They contributed to the economy but had no political rights. The compromise reached was that three-fifths of the slave population would be counted as part of the population for this purpose. Article I Section 2 of the Constitution (before it was amended by the Fourteenth Amendment) was to provide that:

> Representatives [in the House of Representatives] and direct Taxes shall be apportioned among the several States . . . according to their respective Numbers, which shall be determined by adding to the whole Number of free Persons, including those bound to Service for a Term of Years,[19] and excluding Indians not taxed, three fifths of all other Persons [i.e., slaves].

The fugitive slave clause (Article IV, section 2, clause 3 of the Constitution) was proposed on August 28 and approved on August 29. It required a slave who had escaped into another State to be returned to the slave's owner, even if the State into which the slave had escaped had abolished slavery.

As to the executive branch of the new government, the main issues were: would it comprise one person, or more; what would be its powers (including would it have any veto over proposed legislation, and would it be supervised by Congress?); and how would the executive or members of the executive be appointed?

As we have seen, the context for the debate included that: in America it was widely believed that George III's manipulation of the executive branch had corrupted the British constitution and been a significant cause of the War; many of the State constitutions had powerful legislatures and weak executives; and under the Articles, executive authority was exercised by Congress (a model that had not been effective).

On June 1, the Convention began to consider the issues relating to the executive branch. Direct election and appointment by either Congress or the Senate alone were all canvassed. On 2 June, Mr. Wilson (Pennsylvania) proposed an electoral college system, but with electorates for the members of the college being specially determined districts, not States. On June 4 it was resolved that the executive should be a single person. Also, on June 4, the Convention decided to give the Executive a qualified veto over legislation (Article I Section 7 provides for a Presidential veto which can be overridden by two-thirds of Congress). On July 20 it was decided that the Executive should be removeable on impeachment.[20]

On the extent of the Executive's powers; how the Executive would be elected, and for what terms; and whether an Executive would be eligible for re-election, the Convention changed its mind several times during the debates of June and July. These issues would not be resolved until the Convention was considering the text of a draft constitution, from August 6.

As we have seen, in England a fundamental constitutional issue that had been addressed in Magna Carta, the Parliamentary rebellion against Charles I, and the English Revolution, was that Parliament and not the king controlled the power to raise revenue or supply. The President's power to veto bills did not differentiate between supply or appropriation bills, and other bills. Such a distinction was not discussed. The possibility of a President vetoing a revenue or appropriation bill as part of a broader negotiation or conflict with Congress does not seem to have occurred to the normally prescient delegates. Perhaps the fact that the English king had never withheld assent from a grant of money explains this.

On August 24 it was resolved that the Executive would be styled "The President of the United States of America."

On August 31, the Convention resolved to refer open questions to a Committee of Eleven, to see whether the Committee could draft and recommend solutions, with the benefit of having heard the debates. The committee had one representative from each State, except for Rhode Island (which had not attended the Convention), and New York (two of its three representatives had attended for six weeks only, and the third, Alexander Hamilton, was not always present). On September 4, the Convention received the report of the Committee of Eleven and began to crunch the outstanding issues relevant to the Presidency. Some of the Committee's recommendations were accepted on September 4, and the rest were accepted subsequently, with some modifications.

The Committee recommended: that candidates for the Presidency must have been born in the United States and be at least thirty-five years old; four-year terms; and that an electoral college be used to choose the President. These recommendations were accepted.

Each State would have the number of members of the electoral college equal to its number of Senators plus its number of members of the House of Representatives. Each State legislature would appoint electors who would vote for two candidates. At least one candidate had to be an inhabitant of another State. It was up to the State legislatures to decide whether they would hold a general election to choose their electors. The initial Constitution did contain the electoral college provision recommended by the Committee of Eleven (with some changes), and the Twelfth Amendment modified the provision in 1804.

The recommended electoral college clause was trying to address issues including that: to maintain a separation of powers, the President should not be chosen by or subject to Congress; it would be difficult in those days for candidates to be well known nationally, and therefore to use a popular national vote; the system needed national and State aspects; and some possible methods of selection were perceived to bring a risk of corruption.

By basing the number of electors in part on the number of members of the House of Representatives, the Committee was allowing weight to the population of each part of the nation, and by basing it in part on the number of Senators it was allowing weight to each State in the federation (as each State would have two senators). This was consonant with the emerging shape of the Constitution: part national, part federal.

The Committee of Eleven also recommended that the President have the power to make treaties (with the consent of two-thirds of the Senate) and appoint the holders of high offices and judges of the United States (with the consent of the Senate). The consent requirements were checks on the Executive. To those delegates who objected to the legislature having any role in executive appointments because it caused a mixing of executive and legislative powers, according to Madison's notes of September 7, Gouverneur Morris (Pennsylvania[21]) pithily retorted: ". . . as the President was to nominate, there would be responsibility, and as the Senate was to concur, there would be security."[22] Meaning that as the President would select and oversee a nominee, the President could not blame Congress for the nominee's behavior or performance; and that having a house of Congress check each nominee would reduce the risk that the President had failed to spot some disabling flaw in a nominee.

The Virginia Plan provided that Congress should be able to negative State legislation in areas of federal power. The Convention agreed without debate or dissent on May 31, but reversed its position on July 17. To the modern reader, the proposed power to negative seems a strange proposition. Surely Congress should not be able to merely assert that its power supersedes the States' in a particular case? A court as a respected independent arbiter should determine such a question? This provision of the Virginia Plan is all the odder because State Courts were already exercising a power of judicial review, making decisions on the constitutionality of State legislation. Later in the Convention debates, many delegates stated that the federal courts would have the power to determine the constitutionality of laws. Some noted that the Council of Revision proposed in the Virginia Plan sat oddly with the judicial review power, as it would give some members of the judiciary an opportunity to consider an initial veto of legislation as members of the Council of Revision, and then to determine the constitutionality of the legislation as judges.

Neither a power for Congress to negative State legislation nor a Council of Revision made it into the final Constitution. The Constitution does not mention how disputes about the constitutionality of laws should be resolved. The Judiciary Act of 1789 was to provide that federal courts could review whether State legislation conflicted with the Constitution, and the Supreme Court decision of *Marbury v. Madison* in 1803 was to confirm that the Court had a power of judicial review of Congressional legislation. (In 1803, James Madison was Secretary of State.)

As the Confederation Government had been an agent of the States, and the States' non-compliance with many of Congress' requisitions had been one of the problems of the Confederation period, the interaction of national and State law was a key issue that had to be resolved. The issue was addressed in three sections of the Constitution: the enumeration of Congress' powers in Article I Section 8 (with residual powers remaining with the States, a position expressly stated in the Tenth Amendment); the prohibitions of State power in Article I Section 10; and the supremacy clause in Article VI, which provided in effect that in the event of inconsistency, Federal law overrode State law: "This Constitution, and the Laws of the United States which shall be made in Pursuance thereof . . . shall be the supreme Law of the Land; and the Judges in every State shall be bound thereby, any Thing in the Constitution or Laws of any State to the Contrary notwithstanding." The supremacy clause was proposed in Paterson's plan. It was moved at the Convention by Luther Martin (Maryland) on July 17 and adopted unanimously.

The final draft of the Constitution was prepared by the Committee of Style and Arrangement, which was appointed on September 8, and delivered its draft on September 12. The members of the Committee were Alexander Hamilton, William Johnson, Rufus King, James Madison and Gouverneur Morris. Gouverneur Morris—who had made more speeches at the Convention than any other delegate—was the principal drafter of the final Constitution.

Like Washington, Benjamin Franklin had brought his immense prestige to the Convention, as a delegate of Pennsylvania. He was eighty-one years old, and on at least one occasion had to have a speech written by him read to the Convention. At some of the most difficult moments in the debates, he had urged mutual respect in searching for the best way forward. On the final day of the Convention (September 17), he observed that while the Constitution may not be perfect: "It . . . astonishes me, Sir, to find this system approaching so near to perfection as it does."[23]

Famously, according to Madison's notes, while others were signing the final document:

Doctr. FRANKLIN looking towards the Presidents Chair, at the back of which a rising sun happened to be painted, observed to a few members near him, that

Painters had found it difficult to distinguish in their art a rising from a setting sun. I have said he, often and often in the course of the Session, and the vicissitudes of my hopes and fears as to its issue, looked at that behind the President without being able to tell whether it was rising or setting: But now at length I have the happiness to know that it is a rising and not a setting Sun.[24]

Thirty-four delegates signed the proposed Constitution. Several delegates had already left the Convention for personal reasons or because they disapproved of the proposed Constitution. Three (Randolph, Gerry, and Mason) refused to sign because they disapproved of the document.

The signed document was sent by George Washington as President of the Convention to the President of Congress under cover of a letter, written by Gouverneur Morris and dated September 17, 1787, which included:

The friends of our country have long seen and desired, that the power of making war, peace, and treaties, that of levying money and regulating commerce, and the correspondent executive and judicial authorities should be fully and effectually vested in the general government of the Union: But the impropriety of delegating such extensive trust to one body of men is evident. Hence results the necessity of a different organization.

It is obviously impracticable in the federal government of these States, to secure all rights of independent sovereignty to each, and yet provide for the interests and safety of all. . . . It is at all times difficult to draw with precision the line between those rights which must be surrendered and those which must be reserved . . .

In all our deliberations on this subject we kept steadily in our view, that which appears to us of the greatest interest in every true American, the consolidation of our Union, in which is involved our prosperity, felicity, safety, perhaps our national existence . . .[25]

It was a letter that elegantly described the need for and context of the proposed new mechanisms of government and the re-allocation of power, without attempting to justify the detail. The fact that the letter bore Washington's signature must have reminded all readers of the precariousness of the Confederation during the War, as well as their hopes for a successful new nation.

Congress received Washington's letter and the draft of the Constitution on September 20, along with a copy of the Convention's resolutions recommending the next steps that should be taken—that the Constitution should be laid before Congress; and then submitted to a specially elected convention in each State, for assent and ratification by the people. The Convention also recommended that the new system should commence when the Constitution was ratified by convention in nine States.

There were both practical and theoretical reasons for wanting to put the Constitution to a general vote. The new system would result in a reduction of State power, so seeking approval from State legislatures or Congress (which was at this time still the agent of the States) would have likely resulted in failure. And as the people were the source of sovereignty for the new system, they needed to endorse it.

As for requiring only nine States to ratify, given that Rhode Island was not participating in the renovation of the Articles, this meant in effect ratification by three quarters of the engaged States. That was tactically shrewd. To require more would have created an incentive for each State to be one of the last to ratify in the hope of extracting concessions, as Maryland had done with the Articles of Confederation. Unanimity was required to amend the Articles, but nobody thought that the new Constitution was merely the amendment of the Articles.

Congress considered the Convention's product on September 28, and after vigorous discussion resolved "Unanimously that the said Report and the resolutions and letter accompanying the same be transmitted to the several legislatures in Order to be submitted to a convention of Delegates chosen in each state by the people thereof."[26] The unanimity was on the resolution to transmit the Report. There was no endorsement of the draft Constitution. What else could Congress do? The Convention had exceeded its terms of reference and proposed a new system of government. It was not within Congress' power to substantively address the draft Constitution, so it sent the document to the States, as the Convention had hoped. Would the States convene ratifying conventions, or refuse to co-operate in the Convention's audacious attempt to revolutionize the American system of government?

RATIFICATION

In just over four months (by February 6, 1788), six States had elected delegates to, and held, conventions. All six conventions had assented to and ratified the proposed Constitution. There was real momentum.

Delaware ratified first, on December 7. Delaware also pitched for the new capital to be carved out of Delaware territory.

The first State with a large population to ratify was Pennsylvania, five days after Delaware. James Wilson, who as a Pennsylvanian delegate to the Constitutional Convention had made a substantial contribution to its debates, was also a delegate to the ratifying convention. He spoke at length, both in explaining the reasoning behind provisions of the Constitution, and in responding to questions and criticisms. He had in his favour three of the great advantages of the leading proponents of the Constitution: that everyone agreed that the Confederation was deeply flawed; that the proponents had deep knowledge about the proposed Constitution and could convincingly explain its benefits; and that no alternative to the Constitution was proposed by its opponents.

New Jersey ratified on December 18; Georgia on January 2; and Connecticut on January 8. Then came the big test of Massachusetts.

Meanwhile the leading advocates for the Constitution were working tirelessly. They were no longer Continentalists—they had re-branded themselves "Federalists." Between October 27, 1787 and August 15, 1788 (by which time eleven States had ratified), Madison, Hamilton and John Jay wrote and had published the eighty-five "Federalist Papers." Which of them wrote some of the Papers is uncertain: fifty-one are commonly attributed to Hamilton, twenty-nine to Madison, and five to Jay. The Papers were all published under the name "Publius" (after Publius Valerius Poplicola, one of the founders of the Roman Republic). Most of them are excellent, some brilliant.

Some topics spanned several Papers. The first Papers focused on security; then commerce and revenue; then defects in the Confederation; then the need for an energetic government; then more detail on features of the new system. The Papers set out what was needed and why the new Constitution was the best solution. They addressed counter arguments. The volume of high-quality arguments was hugely impressive, presumably building confidence in the Federalist cause and tending to overwhelm opponents.

The Papers were first published in New York. Twenty-five were republished outside New York before ratification. New York was a principal target of the papers because its support for the Convention had been weak, and it was one of the most populous States. Its people needed to be persuaded. It ended up ratifying, but only as the eleventh State, so that the question for it was whether it wished to join or be excluded from the new nation.

As for Massachusetts, Boston was for ratification, the west of the State opposed. Samuel Adams had been a political leader in the State since the 1760s. He had played a leading role in the early stages of the rebellion against the British. He initially opposed the new Constitution, as excessively concentrating power in a remote central government. But after a long meeting with Paul Revere, the hero of the War who had ridden to warn the patriots of the approach of British forces at the initial battles of Lexington and Concord, Adams came out in support of the Constitution. Revere was acting as a representative of the tradesmen and workers of Boston, who believed that without the Constitution Boston's commerce would be annihilated.

Governor John Hancock was another important revolutionary leader in Boston, and the man whose signature appears first on the Declaration of

Independence. He negotiated with the Federalists and came out in support of the Constitution when he obtained their assurances that the Constitution would be promptly amended.

On February 6, Massachusetts ratified. But it also recommended nine specified changes to the Constitution, including that:

- "no person shall be tried for any Crime by which he may incur an infamous punishment or loss of life until he be first indicted by a Grand Jury, except in such cases as may arise in the Government & regulation of the Land & Naval forces." This became the Fifth Amendment;
- "in civil actions between Citizens of different States every issue of fact arising in Actions at common law shall be tried by a Jury if the parties or either of them request it." An expanded version of this became the Seventh Amendment; and
- "it be explicitly declared that all Powers not expressly delegated by the aforesaid Constitution are reserved to the several States to be by them exercised." This became the Tenth Amendment.[27]

Then came a setback in the race for nine ratifications. New Hampshire would likely have voted against had its convention not adjourned on February 22. Tracts that opposed the draft Constitution, but not the Federalist Papers, had been published in New Hampshire. The seaboard was generally in favour of ratification, but farmers in the west were not. The Federalists went to work, getting better newspaper coverage and linking the anti-federalist cause to the devastation caused by the depreciation of paper money.

Maryland ratified unconditionally on April 28. South Carolina ratified on May 23, recommending some amendments. One more State was needed, and a new nation would be born.

On June 21, 1788 it happened. New Hampshire ratified. It added a number of recommended amendments, based on those of Massachusetts plus three more, including that:

- "Congress shall make no Laws touching Religion, or to infringe the rights of Conscience." A modified version of this became the First Amendment; and
- "Congress shall never disarm any Citizen unless such as are or have been in Actual Rebellion." A modified version of this became the Second Amendment.[28]

But on the ground, there were two ninth-ratifying States: because Virginia did not know that New Hampshire had ratified and believed that its decision of June 26 was the determining act. News of New Hampshire's prior ratification arrived when the celebrations in Virginia were already under way.

Virginia was the oldest, largest, most populous, and richest State. Without it and the other States that had not yet ratified, the new nation would be stunted, sharing borders with competing nations with a shared language and history. Only three members of Virginia's delegation to the Philadelphia Convention had signed the final document: George Washington, John Blair, and James Madison. George Mason (principal author of Virginia's own Bill of Rights) and Richard Henry Lee thought the document was defective because it did not contain a Bill of Rights; and Edmund Randolph, who had introduced "the Virginia Plan" to the Philadelphia Convention, thought that the Constitution lacked sufficient checks and balances.

Virginia's convention met from June 2 to 27, 1788. Its debates were open to the public. They were vigorous. George Mason and Patrick Henry (widely considered the most compelling orator of the day) thought that it would create too strong a central government; both spoke against ratification. The final vote was eighty-nine in favour, seventy-nine against.

There were fifty operative words in Virginia's ratifying document. But the document was over 2,700 words long. What was the rest of it about?

It purported to reserve a right to annul the Constitution, in accordance with Lockean principles: "Do in the name and in behalf of the People of Virginia declare and make known that the powers granted under the Constitution being derived from the People of the United States may be resumed by them whensoever the [Constitution] shall be perverted to their injury or oppression . . ."[29]

It recommended a Bill of Rights with twenty clauses. And it recommended another twenty amendments to the Constitution.

I have noted that New York was the eleventh State to ratify. North Carolina and Rhode Island did not come on board until after the new President was in office and the First Congress had met, which occurred in early 1789.

As requested by several ratifying conventions, the First Congress under the new Constitution proposed twelve amendments, including what became known as the Bill of Rights in the First to Tenth Amendments. The emphasis in the Bill of Rights is far more heavily on individual rights than was the case with the English Bill of Rights. As we have seen (in chapter 2), the latter had contained a number of provisions concerned with the machinery of government and the interaction of Parliament and the Crown. The machinery of government was settled elsewhere in the US Constitution; and the political centrality of the individual had advanced in the English-speaking world in law, philosophy, and political philosophy since the English Bill of Rights of 1689.

THE INFLUENCE OF BRITISH HISTORY AND SYSTEM

There were many explicit references in the Philadelphia Convention's debates to the constitutional position in Britain. The influence of the British constitution was described as follows by Catherine Drinker Bowen in her *Miracle at Philadelphia*:

> Members were also used to references concerning the British system of government . . . How is it in England? The question was insistent. . . . It was natural enough. Even the youngest man present had been born under the British government; all of them had grown up in the belief that the English government and the English common law comprised the best and freest system on earth. . . . But there were Convention members who would have none of it.[30]

The primary influence of the British constitution on the debates and the drafting of the Constitution was not overt. It was that the British system was already the foundation of the system, culture and philosophy of law and government in the United States. The legal system in the United States was a modified British system. The State Constitutions had in some cases merely Americanised their British charters, and in other cases reconceptualized and adapted British colonial institutions to a republican model. The British system was itself dynamic, and as we have seen it had changed profoundly in the 140 years since the trial and execution of Charles I. The means of that change, known well to all the delegates at Philadelphia, had included rebellion and radical constitutional innovation. Aided by social contract theories of political science, British Americans in the Revolutionary period were doing what the English in England had done a century before—insisting on a system of government that ensured their rights and liberties against the presumptions of a monarch and the British ruling class. But the Framers' solution in 1787 was more comprehensive and revolutionary that any of the English innovations in the earlier period, including the short-lived English republic. It articulated in a single document a new system of government, built on the new principle of popular sovereignty divided between State and national governments.

The principal changes required for the new Constitution were that the new system must have no monarch and no hereditary aristocracy; that it must be partly national and partly federal; and that it must be more democratic than the British system.

The main theoretical innovation was that the new Constitution had the same source of sovereignty as the State Constitutions—the people. As noted in chapter 7, it had been a maxim of political science that there could be no *"imperium in imperio,"* or division of sovereignty. The delegates invented an exception: sovereignty could be functionally divided where the source of sovereignty is the people and not a monarch, and where there is a well-functioning legal system that can arbitrate peacefully on the implementation of the division. They did not articulate their innovation in those terms, but that is the effect of their great work.

The Framers were lucky to come from the most liberal legal and governmental system and culture of the age. Their genius was to so successfully and enduringly adapt that system and culture to American imperatives. They had the confidence to innovate, and the learning and wisdom to benefit from the experience of the colonial, State Constitution-writing, and Confederation periods.

NOTES

1. *Journals of the Continental Congress*. February 21, 1787, Volume 32, p. 74. Library of Congress 1936, HathiTrust Digital Library. Accessed July 2019. https://babel.hathitrust.org/cgi/pt?id=msu.31293104451897&view=1up&seq=92.

2. "Proceedings of Commissioners to remedy Defects of the Federal Government," Annapolis, September 11, 1786. Accessed August 2019. https://avalon.law.yale.edu/18th_century/annapoli.asp.

3. (Perkins 1994), 173-186.

4. McHenry, James. "Papers of Dr. James McHenry on the Federal Convention of 1787." The Avalon Project, Yale Law School. Accessed August 2019. https://avalon.law.yale.edu/18th_century/mchenry.asp.

5. Madison, James. "Notes on the Debates in the Federal Convention 1787, June 6." Project, Yale Law Schoo. Accessed April 2019. https://avalon.law.yale.edu/18th_century/debates_606.asp.

6. This description draws on a number of sources, but in particular (Ferling 2003), 265-280.

7. Madison, James. "Notes on the Debates in the Federal Convention 1787, May 29." The Avalon Project, Yale Law School. Accessed July 2019. https://avalon.law.yale.edu/18th_century/debates_529.asp.

8. Beeman, Richard. 2009. *Plain, Honest Men: The Making of The American Constitution*. Random House, 98.

9. Madison, James. "Notes on the Debates in the Federal Convention 1787, July 16." The Avalon Project, Yale Law School. Accessed July 2019. https://avalon.law.yale.edu/18th_century/debates_716.asp.

10. (Madison, "Notes on the Debates in the Federal Convention 1787, June 6")

11. In 1812, Mr. Gerry, then Governor of Massachusetts, signed a bill that created new boundaries for State senate electoral districts to benefit his political party. One of the districts in the Boston area was said to resemble the shape of a salamander. The word 'gerrymander' was coined.

12. (Madison, "Notes on the Debates in the Federal Convention 1787, June 6")

13. Madison, James. "Notes on the Debates in the Federal Convention 1787, July 6." The Avalon Project, Yale Law School. Accessed April 2019. https://avalon.law.yale .edu/18th_century/debates_705.asp.

14. ("Constitution of Massachusetts, 1780")

15. Mr. Ellsworth (Connecticut), August 22: "As slaves also multiply so fast in Virginia & Maryland that it is cheaper to raise than import them, whilst in the sickly rice swamps foreign supplies are necessary . . ." Madison, James. "Notes on the Debates in the Federal Convention 1787, August 22." The Avalon Project, Yale Law School. Accessed June 2019. https://avalon.law.yale.edu/18th_century /debates_822.asp.

16. The production of cotton in America was in its infancy. The invention of the cotton-gin by Eli Whitney in 1793-4 was one of the causes of a later boom in production, creating major new demand for slaves.

17. Madison, James. "Notes on the Debates in the Federal Convention 1787, August 21" The Avalon Project, Yale Law School. Accessed August 2019. https:// avalon.law.yale.edu/18th_century/debates_821.asp.

18. (Madison, "Notes on the Debates in the Federal Convention 1787, August 22").

19. "Those bound to Service for a Term of Years" was a reference to immigrants who had obtained their passage to America in return for agreeing to work as indentured servants for several years.

20. Impeachment was a process familiar to the delegates at the Convention, because as we have seen, it was a process that existed in Britain. There are four steps in the current American process to impeach a President. Committees of the House of Representatives conduct an inquiry. The House's Judiciary Committee then considers whether to recommend impeachment. If it does, the House votes on whether to impeach. If the House impeaches, the President is tried by the Senate. If two-thirds of senators who vote are in favour of conviction, the President is convicted and removed from office.

21. Gouverneur Morris was referred to in chapter 6 as representing New York in 1776. He had moved to Pennsylvania since then.

22. Madison, James. "Notes on the Debates in the Federal Convention 1787, September 7." The Avalon Project, Yale Law School. Accessed June 2019. https://avalon .law.yale.edu/18th_century/debates_907.asp.

23. Madison, James. "Notes on the Debates in the Federal Convention 1787, September 17." The Avalon Project, Yale Law School. Accessed June 2019. https:// avalon.law.yale.edu/18th_century/debates_917.asp.

24. Madison, James. "Notes on the Debates in the Federal Convention 1787, September 17."

25. "Letter of the President of the Federal Convention, Dated September 17, 1787, to the President of Congress, Transmitting the Constitution." The Avalon Project, Yale Law School. Accessed August 2019. https://avalon.law.yale.edu/18th_century /translet.asp.

26. *Journals of the Continental Congress*. September 28, 1787. Volume 33, page 549. Library of Congress 1936, HathiTrust Digital Library. Accessed May 2019. https://babel.hathitrust.org/cgi/pt?id=msu.31293020682328&view=1up&seq=177.

27. "Ratification of the Constitution by the State of Massachusetts, February 6, 1788." The Avalon Project, Yale Law School. Accessed May 2019. https://avalon .law.yale.edu/18th_century/ratma.asp.

28. "Ratification of the Constitution by the State of New Hampshire, June 21, 1788." The Avalon Project, Yale Law School. Accessed August 2019. https://avalon .law.yale.edu/18th_century/ratnh.asp.

29. "Ratification of the Constitution by the State of Virginia, June 26, 1788." The Avalon Project, Yale Law School. Accessed April 2019. https://avalon.law.yale .edu/18th_century/ratva.asp.

30. Bowen, Catherine Drinker. 1986: first published in 1966. *Miracle at Philadelphia: the story of the Constitutional Convention May to September 1787*. Back Bay Books, 57.

Epilogue

President Washington declared in his inaugural speech as President that: ". . . the preservation of the sacred fire of liberty and the destiny of the republican model of government are justly considered, perhaps, as "deeply," as "finally," staked on the experiment entrusted to the hands of the American people . . ."[1]

The system of government established by the Constitution is no longer an experiment. It has enabled the great flourishing and freedom of America. The Constitution has also enabled past political exclusion and discrimination to be corrected.

If the Framers themselves regarded the Constitution as an experiment, there is no disrespect to them or their great work in asking whether any amendments would enable the Constitution to better achieve its objects: to promote the general welfare and secure the blessings of liberty.

The Constitution establishes the framework for the government of a huge and culturally, economically, politically, regionally, and socially diverse nation. It does not determine who sits on the Supreme Court or determine the programs or priorities of elected Representatives, Senators, or the President. What it does is to provide a structure within which elected representatives can determine and seek to implement those programs and priorities. The mechanisms are built on certain premises: that people should be free; that government must not be tyrannous; that each branch of government must perform but not overreach its assigned function; and that the general government must be partly federal and partly national. And what government can do is constrained by the Bill of Rights, the First to Tenth Amendments.[2]

We have seen that three reasons for the federal elements of the Constitution were that: the State governments preceded the federal government; travel and communication times in the late eighteenth century required dispersed government; and the economic and cultural differences across the first thirteen Sates made some regional government necessary. Consequently, the Constitution does have several federal elements. Two of those (two Senators for each State, and the way that Electoral College votes are allocated) do favour the residents of less populous States. That seems unfair to many people in the most populous States. But acknowledging and accommodating the regional, cultural, and economic diversity of America was one of the reasons that a federal structure was necessary in 1787. The federal elements do act as a counterweight to the cultural and economic dominance of the large states and metropolitan centres. Reasonable people may differ on whether that counterweight is appropriate, or whether it is unfairly discriminatory against the residents of the most populous States. The Framers themselves disagreed on the extent to which the central government should be federal or national.

A primary objective of the Constitutional system was to protect freedom and thwart tyranny. As noted in chapter 2, at the time of the establishment of the English republic and then at the time of the English Revolution, the tyrant against whom protection was needed was the king, and the means of resisting that tyranny was enhancing the powers of Parliament. But by the time of the American Revolution, Americans believed that Parliament had failed them as the protector of their liberties. So, the Framers were aware that both the Executive branch and the Legislative branch could tend towards tyranny. The Constitution reflects the Framers' ambivalence to both branches: either or both the President and Congress could threaten liberty and good government, so friction between the two would check each of them.

That friction may be used as part of the re-election strategy of a first-term President or of a member of Congress. Dealings between the President and Congress can lead to deadlocks and shutdowns. Perhaps there is too much friction. One way to reduce it would be to adopt a system under which Congress chose the head of the executive branch (as Parliament chooses the Prime Minister in Britain), and a President was elected as the American Head of State with little political power: an office of dignity which could operate as a representative of the nation and not as a partisan political leader. This method of selection of the head of the executive branch was considered at the Convention. It is difficult to imagine such a dramatic change to the Constitution achieving any political momentum now, for reasons including that the question of how Congress would choose the Prime Minister would immediately arise: should it be by a joint sitting of the House and the Senate (which would mirror the Electoral College system), or the House alone (which would remove any role for elected Senators and remove the extra weight given to the representatives of less populous States)?

The issues considered above (the extent of federal representation, and the extent of friction between the President and Congress) are both structural constitutional issues, and it would require substantial amendment to the Constitution to address them.

Are there reforms which would enhance the functioning of America's system of government without materially changing the structure of that system? They might include:

- reforming campaign financing (to reduce the disproportionate political influence of wealthy individuals, corporations, unions, and lobby groups);
- reducing gerrymandering (to make more House electoral districts contestable, so that more candidates would have to pitch to independent and moderate voters, and not just to the most energized partisan voters); and
- improving the conduct of elections (to make it easy for all eligible voters to register and vote, and to ensure that there is confidence in the integrity of the voting and vote-counting processes).

None of these three changes would require substantial or structural changes to the Constitution. The first (reform of campaign financing) would require an amendment which would qualify the First Amendment. The First Amendment has been held by the Supreme Court to significantly constrain limits on campaign and related finance. The second (reducing gerrymandering) would require an amendment to give the Supreme Court a power to review House electoral district boundaries drawn by the States, or an amendment which vested responsibility for drawing those boundaries in an independent body which would determine district boundaries on the basis of principles other than advantaging specific candidates. The third change (improving the conduct of elections) might require an amendment vesting the administration of elections in the national government (preferably in a body which was not subject to control by politicians).

Of course, some people propose more substantial amendments than those mentioned here. Some even argue that an entirely new constitution should be adopted. The Constitution was revolutionary when adopted partly because it sought to distribute power in a way which would make it difficult for any one interest or faction in the nation to dominate its political life. It is not surprising that Americans looking for radical change in the way their country is governed advocate for substantial changes to, or the replacement of, the Constitution. The present Constitution is not conducive to radical political change.

The possible reforms briefly described above would not be fundamental changes to the system of American government. They are mentioned here, and have each often been mentioned elsewhere, as changes that may improve the functioning of the current system while remaining true to its core objects of resisting tyranny, promoting the general welfare, and securing the blessings of liberty, through a representative republican system which is partly federal and partly national.

NOTES

1. (Washington, "First inaugural address as President" 1789)
2. The Bill of Rights must be interpreted and enforced by the Courts. This is a consequence of the Framers embedding the Bill of Rights in the Constitution, thereby excluding it from Congress's legislative power. It can only be amended by amending the Constitution or, in practice, by non-originalist interpretation by the Courts.

Appendix 1

The Legal Status of the Colonies

The following table shows the legal status under British law of each colony when it was established and at the time of independence in 1776.

Table Appendix 1. The Legal Status of the Colonies

Colony	Year legally established	Legal status when established	Legal status in 1776	Other[a]
Virginia	1606	Chartered company colony	Crown (from 1624)	–
Massachusetts	1629	Chartered company colony	Crown (from 1684, with charter 1691–1774)	Charter for New England 1620, Charter for Massachusetts Bay 1629.
Maryland	1632	Proprietary	Proprietary	Rebel government 1689–92, Royal government 1692–1715.
Connecticut	1662	Chartered company colony	Chartered company colony	White settlement began in 1636[b].
North Carolina	1663	Proprietary (as part of Carolina)	Crown (from 1729)	Royal governor from 1712.
Rhode Island	1663	Chartered company colony	Chartered company colony	White settlement began in 1636.

(continued)

Table Appendix 1. *(continued)*

Colony	Year legally established	Legal status when established	Legal status in 1776	Other[a]
South Carolina	1663	Proprietary (as part of Carolina)	Crown (from 1729)	Royal governor from 1719.
Delaware	1664	Proprietary	Proprietary	Part of New Netherlands before 1664, then part of New York. Granted to William Penn in 1682. Penn granted it a charter in 1701.
New Jersey	1664	Proprietary	Crown (from 1702)	Part of New Netherlands before 1664, granted to the Duke of York in 1664. He sold it to two proprietors, who granted it a charter in 1664.
New York	1664	Proprietary	Crown (from 1685)	Part of New Netherlands before 1664, granted to Duke of York 1664. He became king in 1685.
New Hampshire	1679	Crown, with charter	Crown, with charter	Land grants from 1620s.
Pennsylvania	1681	Proprietary	Proprietary	–
Georgia	1732	Proprietary, to Trustees	Crown (from 1752)	Split from South Carolina.

Source: Table prepared by the author using the charters and related documents at "Colonial Charters, Grants and Related Documents" in the Avalon Project of the Yale Law School Lillian Goldman Law Library, http://avalon.law.yale.edu/subject_menus/statech.asp viewed through November 2018 to July 2020, and using other sources cited in Chapters 1, 2, 5 and 6.

a. In this column, I have not mentioned the charters for colonies which included the areas of Connecticut, Rhode Island, and New Hampshire before those areas became separate colonies under English law because, until then, those colonies were officially governed from Plymouth or Boston.

b. The Fundamental Orders of 1639 were adopted by settlers, purporting to establish a new Commonwealth with the Orders as its constitutional document. Their legal validity under English law was doubtful, so I have treated the Charter of 1662 as the document that legally established the colony.

Appendix 2

1790 Census Data

The immediate causes of the Revolution began in 1763 and the Revolutionary period ended in 1788 with ratification of the Constitution, but there are no census data for that period. The first census data are from 1790.

Appendix 2

Table Appendix 2. 1790 Census Data

District	Free white males 16+ years	Free white males 16– years	Free white females	All other free persons	Slaves	Total– 1790 census
Connecticut	60,523	54,403	117,448	2,808	2,764	**237,946**
Delaware	11,783	12,143	22,384	3,899	8,887	**59,096**
Georgia	13,103	14,044	25,739	398	29,264	**82,548**
Kentucky [a]	15,154	17,057	28,922	114	12,430	**73,677**
Maine [a]	24,384	24,748	46,870	538	0	**96,540**
Maryland	55,915	51,339	101,395	8,043	103,036	**319,728**
Massachusetts	95,453	87,289	190,582	5,463	0	**378,787**
N. Hampshire	36,086	34,851	70,160	630	158	**141,885**
New Jersey	45,251	41,416	83,287	2,762	11,423	**184,139**
New York	83,700	78,122	152,320	4,654	21,324	**340,120**
North Carolina	69,988	77,506	140,710	4,975	100,572	**393,751**
Pennsylvania	110,788	106,948	206,363	6,537	3,737	**434,373**
Rhode Island	16,019	15,799	32,652	3,407	948	**68,825**
South Carolina	35,576	37,722	66,880	1,801	107,094	**249,073**
Southwest Territory [a]	6,271[b]	10,277[b]	15,365	361	3,417	**35,691**
Vermont [a]	22,435	22,328	40,505	255	16	**85,539**
Virginia	110,936	116,135	215,046	12,866	292,627	**747,610**
Total	**813,365**	**802,127**	**1,556,628**	59,511	697,697	3,929,328

Source: 1790 USA census data.

a. Kentucky, Maine, the Southwest Territory, and Vermont were not British colonies and then founding States during the Revolutionary period. In 1763 they were part of Virginia, Massachusetts, North Carolina, and New Hampshire and New York respectively. No data from 1790 were published for the Northwest Territory.
b. In the Southwest Territory, 21 years and not 16 years of age was used to determine the two age categories of free white males.

Appendix 3

The Origins of the Common Law

Injustice enrages us. It leads to feuds, revenge, and violence. Without justice personal rights are uncertain, safety is at risk, corruption is higher, economic development is difficult, and power is concentrated in the hands of bullies or worse.

People can only be free and empowered when rules are fair, known, and predictably enforced. In a society where there is power without known rules, or where rules are arbitrarily or capriciously enforced, the safest course is to always please those in power. That is not freedom.

A core function of good government is to provide justice. The preamble to the Constitution of the United States provides that: "We the People of the United States, in Order to form a more perfect Union, *establish Justice* [emphasis added], insure domestic Tranquility, provide for the common defence, promote the general Welfare, and secure the Blessings of Liberty to ourselves and our Posterity, do ordain and establish this Constitution for the United States of America."

Establishing justice is one specific objective, but without it, there would be no "domestic Tranquility," "general Welfare," or "Blessings of Liberty." Justice underpins four of the six objectives of the Constitution. Its importance is profound and fundamental.

Their legal systems have been essential to the development of the remarkable freedom and prosperity which some English-speaking countries have enjoyed in recent times. The common law is a foundation of law in those countries.

In the United States after the Revolution, the States adopted the common law through provisions in their constitutions or by specific statutes. At the federal/national level, the adoption of the common law was implied (and in some respects modified) by the Constitution.

The "common law" has at least two meanings. In historical texts, it can mean "the law that applies throughout England," or that is common to all of England. But the usual current meaning of "common law" is "law based on judges' decisions, and not law made by legislation"[1].

Sometimes the common law is described as "judge made law." That description is based on a misunderstanding of how the common law was in fact made. "Law based on judges' decisions" is more cumbersome but more accurate. Judges did not sit as legislators and decide the law, as "judge made law" implies. They made the best decisions that they could on the facts of the individual cases that they were considering.

The general principles of common law are derived from accumulated judicial decisions, or precedents. These principles were often described late in the development of the common law. Principles were generalised distillations of judges' reasoning in prior individual cases.

In the common law system when a judge encounters a new problem in a case, to do justice in that case the judge's solution may include an adaptation or refinement of principle, or even something new. This may appear to be making new law. But if the judge is following the common law method, the new element will be an attempt to correctly apply existing precedent to the novel problem in the case.

In the early days of the development of the common law, any of the following factors could influence the common law judges' decisions:

- the customs of people in the place where the facts of the case had occurred;
- questions asked by, and the decisions of, juries;
- the legal form in which cases were pleaded;
- interactions between Lords' Courts, County Courts, and the Monarch's Courts;
- interactions with the Church and with Chancery; and
- most importantly, precedent, or prior decisions made by judges in similar cases.

How did the common law begin to develop? In different ways, depending on the area of law. I will briefly describe land law, criminal law, and the law of wrongs (or tort).[2]

William the Conqueror (reigned 1066–87) introduced the feudal system in England. He confiscated land from Anglo-Saxon owners who did not submit to him and granted much of it to his followers and supporters, mostly Normans. There were about one hundred and seventy of them after the Conquest. The rest of the land was retained by the King or granted to the Church.

The essence of a feudal system is that the lords and barons who enjoy the benefit of holding land from the king (the "tenants in chief") are under obligations to the king to perform services. Most importantly, they are required to serve the king as knights, and to provide other knights and soldiers, as well as armor, weaponry, and supplies.

The legal principle required to make this system work was that all rights in land were derived from a grant from the king. The conditions of service were not just patched on to an underlying or pre-existing right to the land—they were an integral and inseparable part of the package. The king used his primary ownership of all land (acquired by right of conquest) to obtain loyalty and services.

Over time, the importance of the feudal obligations declined, and the right to land morphed from being dependent on the discharge of obligations to being unconditional—what we would call ownership. Services were then bought by the king with money, rather than being provided to satisfy conditions attached to the occupation of land.

Land was the most important asset class at the time, and agriculture was the largest industry. People are unlikely to forego present consumption and invest in the hope of future returns if their property rights are not enforceable and they may lose the assets in which they have invested. The firming-up of property rights over time was an important enabler and pre-condition of economic development.

In feudal times, the lords and barons granted to other people rights to land in which the lords and barons had rights from the king. Those subsidiary rights were also subject to obligations of service. A knight who did not hold land from the king might hold a manor from a lord or baron and be required by the lord or baron to serve as a knight and provide other knights or soldiers when the lord or baron was called on to discharge his obligation to the king. Again, the knight's claim to the land was subject to conditions of service and was not ownership in the modern sense. There were about six thousand manors after the Conquest. Those who held manors, in turn, granted interests in land which were conditional on services—principally the provision of agricultural labor.

It is conceptually wrong to think of many rights to assets under the feudal system as property rights. Many were only expectations, based on custom. We would regard the following as key attributes of ownership: without the consent or approval of anyone else, the owner can sell an owned asset and keep the proceeds of sale or deal with the asset in other ways as he or she chooses. Feudal interests in land usually failed that test.

The king kept records of which lords or barons held which land by grant from him. The lords or barons kept records of who held which land from them. So did the knights who held manors. Astonishingly, as recently as 1925 "much English land was still classed as 'copyhold,' so named because the only document of title you could have was a copy of . . . the record of the manor court."[3] Changes made by the Reform Act of 1832 (mentioned in chapters 2 and 3) included expanding the franchise to include owners of land in copyhold worth at least £10 a year.

The North American colonies did not escape the remnants of the law of feudal land ownership. For example, in royal and proprietary colonies, land holders could be obliged to pay "quitrents" or payments in lieu of notional obligations of service to the king or proprietor, as well as any taxes levied by the colonial government.

If rights to land cascaded down from the king and were initially all contingent on service, what happened on the death of a landholder? How was the next contingent landholder chosen?

At first after the Conquest, the question of who would be the next landholder was determined by custom in the court of the person who had granted the interest in land. The king or the king's courts made decisions in respect of the lords or barons who held their rights by grant from the king. For other land, the relevant court was the court of the lord or knight who had granted the interest in land.

Henry II (reigned 1154–89) was sufficiently concerned about poor decisions by these local courts that he gave the royal courts a supervisory jurisdiction over local courts in land law cases. Someone claiming to have been wrongly dispossessed of their land, or to be a rightful heir who had not succeeded or could not claim in the lord's court, could bring the claim in the King's court. This enabled more systematic and consistent decisions about rights to land.

The common law rules regarding land started as the criteria for choosing the next landholder and were heavily influenced by custom. At first, the custom was that the next landholder was the dead man's eldest son, unless he was not fit for discharging the conditions of service. In the case of land held by a knight, the eldest son could be passed over if a younger son was a better knight.

As the money economy developed and the importance of the conditions of service attached to land reduced, and with elder sons being able to take their cases to the king's court, the eldest son's expectation of inheritance became more secure. The king's court was more likely to apply firm rules, and not exercise discretion based on local factors or the individual characteristics of claimants. Landholders were starting to become landowners, and not just holders subject to service obligations during their lives and the local lord's decision on their death.

The story of the development of English land law is immensely convoluted. Interests in land could become complex, relying on common law but also on Chancery (the Lord Chancellor's court) and the law of trusts, and future rights in land could be created.

The inflexibility of the common law in some areas was one of its limitations. This was partly a function of the importance of specific and inflexible pleadings that were available in the old common law courts. Cases were decided in the context of those pleadings, not by the application of substantive principles of law.

The Lord Chancellor's court could give more flexible remedies than the common law courts. The Chancery court's function was to provide just and equitable results on the cases before it. It developed the branch of English law commonly referred to as equity. The judges in the Court of Chancery did not apply the common law. They applied principles of fairness, or equity.

In recent times, land law has been supplemented by legislation. But most of the development of the great body of substantive land law occurred in the courts, with litigants pressing for flexibility and certainty, and judges deciding the cases before them, one by one. The cumulative results of those decisions were first summarized in the first textbook of English law, *Littleton's Tenures*, published in 1481. The cumulative results of modern land law have been summarized in textbooks from the mid-nineteenth century.

Even today there are echoes of the feudal origins of land law in England and countries that have taken their land law from it. For example, freehold title is still commonly referred to by lawyers in some jurisdictions as "fee simple," which is a term of feudal origin meaning a holding which is not subject to obligations or restrictions on transfer. Other forms of holding could be subject to obligations or restrictions and would be designated as another form of "fee."

England's common law for criminal matters began not with feudal concepts, but with decline in the belief that criminal guilt could be revealed by the outcome of combat or ordeals. Such tests had been considered a more reliable way of ascertaining guilt than relying on the testimony of the injured party or the accused.

If the accuser claimed to have witnessed an alleged crime, the accuser could in some cases swear an oath. If the accused denied the charge, the oath would be tested by combat. Judicial combat was not practiced in England before the Conquest, although it was widespread in Europe. William the Conqueror ordered that the English were not required to submit to it, so it was used only between Normans.

If there was direct evidence that an alleged crime had been committed but no direct evidence of who had committed it, the accused could plead guilty or swear an oath of denial. That oath would be tested by ordeal. If there was no direct evidence of the crime, the accused's oath could be tested by compurgation—neighbors supporting the accused's oath by swearing to the accused's good character.

Ordeal usually involved lowering the accused into water and seeing whether he sank or floated, or requiring him to carry hot irons and examining his wounds several days later. A priest was required to pronounce the outcome of the ordeal. Ordeal was not available after 1215, when the Church ceased to participate in the practice because Church reformers regarded it as irrational.

Before the Conquest, juries had been used in England to settle disputes at a local level, probably beginning in the Danelaw (the part of eastern England north of the Thames where the Vikings' law had prevailed), but juries were also in use outside the Danelaw. The jury system emerged in all of England to replace combat, compurgation, and ordeal.

Before Henry II's reforms, groups of citizens had already had some functions in fact-finding in land law cases and in the enforcement of the criminal law. Henry II's Assize of Clarendon of 1166 introduced a "jury of presentment," whose members were bound to declare on oath whether any local man had committed the relevant crime. The "Statute of Westminster" of 1275 made the use of a jury compulsory in all criminal cases.

In Europe, courts were also moving away from the old methods of proof— trial by combat and ordeal. But there, procedure based on Roman and canonical law replaced the old methods. Judges decided questions of fact as well as of law. They carried out interrogations in person. Witnesses, confessions, secret hearings, and torture were all used. Learned Continental lawyers had nothing but contempt for juries.

The jury system was an aspect of the institutions of government that developed in England that kept the system in touch with the views of the people (initially men from the higher classes, but broadening over time), rather than becoming the monopoly of an elite profession.

The roles of judges and juries were different from their modern roles in criminal trials. Now, the jury is the tribunal of fact—it decides on whether the facts required to establish the elements of the legal test of guilt occurred "beyond reasonable doubt." Now, the jury does not decide questions of law such as: what comprise the elements of the legal test of guilt, and what defenses may be available to the accused.

But in the early days of jury trials, the jury simply determined whether the accused was guilty or not. Facts and law were not separately identifiable components of the jury's decision. The jury was not required to give reasons. Juries applied their own views on the justice of the cases before them.

Conscientious juries in difficult cases did ask judges for guidance on the principles that they should apply, and records survive of some of those questions and the directions that judges gave in response. If a judge were not sure how to answer a jury's question, he could hold the case over and consult with colleagues when he was back in London. When he was next at the place of the trial, the judge would direct the jury on the issue about which the jury had asked its question. The jury would then determine whether the accused was guilty or not guilty.

It is through this process of giving directions to juries in response to questions from them that judges began to develop and articulate principles which became the foundations of the English criminal law.

The king's government had no role in policing. Policing was organized by local communities. If a crime was committed, the "hue and cry" was raised (by yelling). Men were required to have weapons nearby, and to be ready to pursue suspects. A private suit was brought at the next county court. The accused was summoned. If he did not appear, he was outlawed.

Legislation was passed during Edward I's reign to improve policing. The "Statute of Winchester" of 1285 imposed an obligation on local communities to detain felons and robbers, and to require that: walled towns shut their gates at night and have night watchmen; the land on each side of highways be cleared for two hundred feet; arms be kept; and the hue and cry be followed.

From the time of Henry II, the trial of a crime involving violence would wait until a royal judge visited the locality. The king had jurisdiction because violent crimes involved a breach of the king's peace. Non-violent crimes (mostly crimes of dishonesty) were still dealt with by local courts.

During Edward I's reign (reigned 1272–1307) the ability of judges to consult with informed colleagues and the depth of expertise available for the development of the common law advanced. Judges became full-time specialists. The right to appear in court as a lawyer was made conditional on legal knowledge. The Inns of Court, originally residential communities of lawyers, began to develop in London.

Today in England criminal offences include common law offences, legislated offences that codify or modify earlier common law offences, and legislated offences that do not have an antecedent in common law. The last category, in recent times, included European Union regulation.

As for the law relating to evidence and the procedures to be used in criminal trials—all vital in conducting a trial—the position is the same: there is a mixture of uncodified common law, codified or modified common law, and legislated provisions.

For our purposes, what is relevant is how the system got going. Guidance on how to deal with the problems that juries identified was given to the juries by judges at the juries' request. We do not know to what extent juries accepted the judges' directions, because the juries returned their verdicts but did not give reasons. The issues were framed by juries through the questions that they chose to ask. The judges' directions in response, if recorded, influenced parties in subsequent cases where the same issues arose.

Initially after the Conquest, the King had less interest in civil claims (claims not involving an alleged crime): such matters as trespass, compensation for injury, repayment of debt, and breach of contract. These matters stayed in local courts for longer.

A way to get a civil claim in front of a royal court was to allege that the relevant event included a breach of the king's peace. If a breach of the king's peace was alleged a jury was required. In the early fourteenth century breaches of the king's peace were being fictitiously alleged by plaintiffs to invoke the jurisdiction of the royal courts. Defendants could not deny the fiction, because the judge would say that whether the facts alleged were correct was a matter for the jury, and the jury would have no interest in the fiction but would decide the case on its merits.

In a case in 1317 a buyer of wine claimed that the seller had diluted the wine with saltwater. The plaintiff alleged that this was done against the king's peace and with force of arms. The jury focused on the condition of the wine and was not troubled with the fiction about the breach of the peace.

In another case the owner of a horse who was suing a blacksmith for killing the horse pleaded simply that the horse was killed by the defendant in breach of the king's peace, without even mentioning that the horse was in the defendant's possession because he was a blacksmith performing a service for the owner.

From late in the fourteenth century all tort actions came before the king's court and the need to use the fiction of a breach of the king's peace fell away. Tort cases continued to be heard using a jury.

Civil cases before the king's court were begun in Westminster, and that is where judgment was given. The key issues in a case were however considered by a jury in the country, with the verdict being reported back to Westminster. So, each case had three phases: begun in Westminster, decision by a jury in the country, and judgment in Westminster.

The parties were represented by lawyers in civil cases (they were not in criminal cases). The plaintiff's lawyer would try to make sure that the court in Westminster put the right question to the jury in the country, and so would focus on the pleading of the case and try to be allowed to make a special pleading which defined the issues in the case more clearly than a general pleading. Plaintiffs' lawyers had limited success with this, and juries did not articulate what principles or tests they applied in reaching their verdicts.

Between the fifteenth and sixteenth centuries, there was more progress in developing tort law principles. Pleading was no longer oral but done by exchanging papers. This led to more precision.

When the verdict from the country was reported back to the court in Westminster, the lawyers could argue the consequences of the verdict, and whether the direction to the jury had been correct. The jury's verdict could not be revisited or challenged by the lawyers or the judge, but verdicts implied approaches to issues such as responsibility, intention or excuse which influenced lawyers when later pleading or arguing similar cases.

Because the common law originated with input from juries, it is grounded in the world as it is (or, in some cases, was). It is not Parliament's law. To some degree, it is the people's law.[4] This point must be qualified by noting that the common law can be changed by legislation. Sometimes such changes may codify, clarify, or update the common law. On other occasions, legislated changes may substitute different law for the law based on judges' decisions.

In some areas of law such changes in recent decades have been so extensive that the residue of the law based on judges' decisions is slight, and the continuing influence of the common law is mostly in the way that the lawyers frame their submissions based on earlier decisions by judges. It is the common law lawyer's method rather than the common law legal principles that survive.

This method and the fact that the common law is based on precedent encourage lawyers in common law jurisdictions in their individual cases to engage the judge in finding the prior decisions of judges which give the best guidance on how to do justice in the case before the Court. The lawyers (in their pleadings and submissions, and how they present the evidence) and judges work from decisions in similar cases, and not from general propositions that have been legislated.

This feature of how common law lawyers and judges work is consistent with England's evolutionary constitution which adapts to changing circumstances on the ground, rather than imposing a wholly new system or rules from a more abstract source. This adaptive system is self-reinforcing and cannot be found in places which suffer under tyranny, oligarchy or other systems of government which treat people as the objects of the activity of government rather than (to some degree) participants in their own government.

In the common law system when a judge encounters a new problem in a case, in order to do justice in the case his or her solution may include something new. And in a system of law which starts with codified rules made by a king or legislator, a judge hearing a case may have to apply something new in applying the legislated rule to the individual case. In any legal system judges will play this role. Laws can never be articulated to deal in advance with every conceivable fact scenario. Laws are to varying degrees generalized.

In both systems lawyers and judges can play an active role in influencing how the law is interpreted and applied. But this does not negate the difference in the origins and method between the two systems. It is still true, and significant, that in the common law world the judges' decisions become the precedents which influence how later cases will be decided. Initially judges made those decisions not as law makers but as deciders of cases, based on custom; questions asked by, and the decisions of, juries; the legal form in which cases had been pleaded; interaction with the equity courts; and, increasingly over time, precedent or decisions made by other judges in similar cases.

NOTES

1. In England and some other jurisdictions, a nuance to this second meaning is that in technical legal texts "common law" is likely to refer to law based on judges' decisions from the Monarch's courts and not to law based on judges' decisions in "equity" courts (originally the courts of Chancery). In ordinary usage "common law" is likely to include both kinds of law based on judges' decisions.

2. This Appendix describes a system of law which by the time of the American Revolution had evolved over some seven hundred years. The primary records of the development of the common law are the records of case pleadings and judges' decisions over that period. In writing this Appendix, I have drawn mainly from secondary sources: the work of legal scholars. My sources are set out in the Bibliography and Further Reading sections of this book. I am particularly indebted to Milsom, S. F. C. 2003. *A Natural History of the Common Law*. Columbia University Press and Caenegem, R. C. van. 1973. *The Birth of the English Common Law*. Cambridge University Press.

3. (Milsom 2003), p 56.

4. Which people? That depends on the area of law. If a case was about interests in land, people with no such interests were not involved. If a case were about murder or injury to a person, it could involve people who had no property.

Bibliography

1790 USA census data. Thomas Jefferson as Secretary of State, viewed at the United States Census Bureau's website. Accessed November 2018 to July 2020. https://www.census.gov/programs-surveys/decennial-census/decade/decennial-publications.1790.html.

Acemoglu, Daron and Robinson, James A. 2012. *Why Nations Fail: the Origins of Power, Prosperity, and Poverty*. Crown Business.

"Act of Abjuration of 1581" (Dutch). *The Library of Original Sources*, ed Thatcher, Oliver J. University Research Extension Co., c1907, Volume 5, page 190. Internet Archive. Accessed June 2018 to July 2020. https://archive.org/details/libraryoforigina05thatuoft/page/190/mode/2up.

"Act of the Commons of England Assembled in Parliament, for Erecting of a High Court of Justice, for the Trying and Judging of Charles Stuart, King of England." January 1649. *Acts and Ordinances of the Interregnum, 1642–1660*, ed. C. H. Firth and R. S. Rait (London, 1911), pp. 1253–1255. British History Online. Accessed July 2018 to July 2020. http://www.british-history.ac.uk/no-series/acts-ordinances-interregnum/pp1253-1255.

"Agreement between the Settlers at New Plymouth, 1620." The Avalon Project, Yale Law School. Accessed March 2019. https://avalon.law.yale.edu/17th_century/mayflower.asp.

"Albany Plan of Union, 1754." The Avalon Project, Yale Law School. Accessed September 2018 to July 2020. https://avalon.law.yale.edu/18th_century/albany.asp.

The Anglo-Saxon Chronicle (Late ninth century). Translation by Rev. James Ingram 1823. Everyman Press, 1912, London. Accessed August 2018. Internet Archive: https://archive.org/stream/Anglo-saxonChronicles/anglo_saxon_chronicle_djvu.txt.

"Articles of Confederation as presented to Congress." *Journals of the Continental Congress*, July 12, 1777, Volume 5 page 546. Library of Congress 1906. Accessed January 2019. https://memory.loc.gov/cgi-bin/ampage?collId=lljc&fileName=00.

"Articles of Confederation." The Avalon Project, Yale Law School. Accessed October 2018 to July 2020. https://avalon.law.yale.edu/18th_century/artconf.asp.

"Articles of Impeachment of King Charles I, 1649." *The Trial of Charles I*, edited by Lockyer, Roger; London: The Folio Society; 1959; pp. 82–85. Accessed July 2018 to July 2020. https://en.wikisource.org/wiki/Articles_of_Impeachment_of_King _Charles_I.

Bagehot, Walter. 1878. *The English Constitution*. C. Kegan Paul & Co.

Beeman, Richard. 2009. *Plain, Honest Men: The Making of The American Constitution*. Random House.

Bourke, Stephen. 1991. "Subordinate Rule Making—An Historical Perspective." *Admin Review*, a newsletter of the Australian Administrative Review Council. Accessed October 2018. http://classic.austlii.edu.au/au/journals/AdminRw/1991/2 .pdf viewed.

Bowen, Catherine Drinker. 1986: first published 1966. *Miracle at Philadelphia: the story of the Constitutional Convention May to September 1787*. Back Bay Books.

Bragg, Melvyn. 2012. *The Book of Books*. Hodder & Stoughton.

Broadberry, S., Campbell, B., Klein, A., Overton, M., & Van Leeuwen, B. 2015. *British Economic Growth, 1270–1870*. Cambridge University Press. doi:10.1017/ CBO9781110770760.

Broadberry, Stephen; Guan, Hanhui; and Li, David Daokui. 2017. "China, Europe And The Great Divergence: A Study In Historical National Accounting, 980– 1850." (University of Oxford, *Discussion Papers in Economics and Social History*, Number 155 April 2017). Accessed October 2018. https://www.economics.ox.ac .uk/materials/working_papers/2839/155aprilbroadberry.pdf.

"Bubble Act 6 George I c18" (1719). *The Statutes at Large of England and of Great-Britain*. edited by Raithby, John London 1811. Volume 8 page 322 and following. Accessed October 2018. https://books.google.ca/books?id=BYlKAAAAYAAJ&lp g=PA372&ots=ujx1vUF28B&pg=PA322#v=onepage&q&f=false.

Caenegem, R. C. van. 1973. *The Birth of the English Common Law*. Cambridge University Press.

"Charles II, 1660: An Act of Free and Generall Pardon Indempnity and Oblivion." *Statutes of the Realm*: Volume 5, 1628–80, ed. John Raithby (s.l, 1819), pp. 226–234. British History Online. Accessed July 2018 to September 2018. http://www.british -history.ac.uk/statutes-realm/vol5/pp226-234.

"Charter of Carolina, 1663." The Avalon Project, Yale Law School. Accessed August 2018 to July 2020. https://avalon.law.yale.edu/17th_century/nc01.asp.

"Charter of Massachusetts Bay, 1691." The Avalon Project, Yale Law School. Accessed March 2019 to July 2020. https://avalon.law.yale.edu/17th_century/mass07. asp.

"Charter for the Province of Pennsylvania, 1681." The Avalon Project, Yale Law School. Accessed March 2019 to July 2020. https://avalon.law.yale.edu/17th _century/pa01.asp.

"Colonial Charters, Grants and Related Documents." Avalon Project of the Yale Law School Lillian Goldman Law Library. Accessed November 2018 to July 2020. http://avalon.law.yale.edu/subject_menus/statech.asp.

"Constitution of Massachusetts, 1780." George Mason University, Antonin Scalia Law School. Accessed July 2019. https://www.law.gmu.edu/assets/files/academics/founders/Mass-Constitution.pdf.

"Constitution of New York, 1777." The Avalon Project, Yale Law School. Accessed October 2018 to July 2020. https://avalon.law.yale.edu/18th_century/ny01.asp.

"Constitution of Virginia. June 29, 1776." The Avalon Project at Yale Law School, but diverted to George Mason University's Antonin Scalia Law School's website. Accessed October 2018 to July 2020. https://www.law.gmu.edu/assets/files/academics/founders/VA-Constitution.pdf.

"Copies of Two Papers written by the Late King Charles II together with a Copy of a Paper written by the late Duchess of York." Volume 2: February 5, 1685–December 8, 1688, in *Calendar of Treasury Papers*, Volume 1, 1556–1696, ed. Joseph Redington (London, 1868), pp. 15–31. British History Online. Accessed August 2018. http://www.british-history.ac.uk/cal-treasury-papers/vol1/pp15-31.

"Declaration and Resolves of the First Continental Congress, October 14, 1774." The Avalon Project, Yale Law School. Accessed November 2018 to July 2020. https://avalon.law.yale.edu/18th_century/resolves.asp.

"Declaration by the Representatives of the United Colonies of North-America, Now Met in Congress at Philadelphia, Setting Forth the Causes and Necessity of Their Taking Up Arms." p.168 Morison, Samuel Eliot and Henry Steele Commager, William E. Leuchtenburg. *The Growth of the American Republic*: Volume 1. Seventh Edition. New York : Oxford University Press; 1980. Accessed August 2018 to July 2020. The Avalon Project, Yale Law School https://avalon.law.yale.edu/18th_century/arms.asp.

"Declaration of Independence, 1776." The Avalon Project, Yale Law School. Accessed November 2018 to July 2020. https://avalon.law.yale.edu/18th_century/declare.asp.

"Declaration of Indulgence of King James II, April 4, 1687." The Jacobite Heritage. Accessed August 2018. https://web.archive.org/web/20040227140532/http://www.jacobite.ca/documents/16870404.htm.

"Declaration of Rights, and the Constitution and Form of Government agreed to by the Delegates of Maryland, in Free and Full Convention Assembled, November 1776." The Avalon Project, Yale Law School. Accessed November 2018 to May 2020. https://avalon.law.yale.edu/17th_century/ma02.asp.

"Declaratory Act, March 18, 1766." The Avalon Project, Yale Law School. Accessed April 2019. https://avalon.law.yale.edu/18th_century/declaratory_act_1766.asp.

de Secondat, C. L., Baron de la Brede et de Montesquieu. 1748. *The Spirit of Laws*. Translated edition University of California Press, 1977.

"English Bill of Rights, 1689. 1 William & Mary Sess 2 c 2." The Avalon Project, Yale Law School. Accessed July 2018 to July 2020. https://avalon.law.yale.edu/17th_century/england.asp.

"Entire ceremonies of the coronations of His Majesty King Charles II and of her Majesty Queen Mary, Consort to James II: As published by those learned heralds Ashmole and Sandford," 1761. Printed for Owen and others. Eighteenth Century Collections Online, University of Michigan, Text Creation Partnership. Accessed

August to December 2018. https://quod.lib.umich.edu/e/ecco/004895348.0001.00
0/1:6.1?rgn=div2;view=toc.

"Examination of Franklin before the Committee of the Whole of the House of Commons, 13 February 1766." National Archives. Accessed March 2019. https://founders.archives.gov/documents/Franklin/01-13-02-0035.

"Factsheet P1 Parliamentary Questions." House of Commons Information Office. Accessed October 15, 2018 to July 2020. https://www.parliament.uk/documents/commons-information-office/p01.pdf.

Ferling, John E. 2003. *A Leap in the Dark: The Struggle to Create the American Republic*. Oxford University Press.

"First Charter of Virginia; April 10, 1606." The Avalon Project, Yale Law School. Accessed March to September 2019. https://avalon.law.yale.edu/17th_century/va01.asp.

Foxe, John. 1563. *Foxe's Book Of Martyrs*. Knight and Son, 1856. Open Library. Accessed August 2018. https://openlibrary.org/books/OL1586721M/Foxe's_book_of_martyrs.

Friel, Ian. 2009. "Elizabethan Merchant Ships and Shipbuilding." Gresham College, lecture at the Museum of London. Accessed August 2018. https://www.gresham.ac.uk/lectures-and-events/elizabethan-merchant-ships-and-shipbuilding.

Fritze, Ronald H., Robison, William B. 1996. *Historical Dictionary of Stuart England, 1603–1689*. William, Greenwood Press.

Gardiner, S. R. (editor). 1906. "Protestation Of The House Of Commons. March 2, 1629," in *The Constitutional Documents of the Puritan Revolution, 1625–1660*. Clarendon Press, 1906, The Online Library Of Liberty. Accessed June to September 2018. http://oll-resources.s3.amazonaws.com/titles/1434/Gardiner_046.

Hamilton, Alexander. 1781. "The Continentalist. No. 1." National Archives. Accessed June 2019. https://founders.archives.gov/documents/Hamilton/01-02-02-1179.

"House of Commons Journal Volume 10: 22 January 1689." *Journal of the House of Commons*: Volume 10, 1688–1693 (London, 1802), pp. 9–12. British History Online. Accessed July 2018. http://www.british-history.ac.uk/commons-jrnl/vol10/pp9-12.

"House of Commons Journal Volume 10: 28 January 1689." *Journal of the House of Commons*: Volume 10, 1688–1693 (London, 1802), p. 14. British History Online. Accessed August 2018 to July 2020. http://www.british-history.ac.uk/commons-jrnl/vol10/p14.

"House of Commons Journal Volume 10: 29 January 1689." *Journal of the House of Commons*: Volume 10, 1688–1693 (London, 1802), pp. 14–15. British History Online. Accessed July to November 2018. https://www.british-history.ac.uk/commons-jrnl/vol10/pp14-15.

"Instrument of Government." American Historical Documents. Original Sources. Accessed August 2018. www.originalsources.com/Document.aspx?DocID=Y9YT23252Q2UKKY.

Journals of the Continental Congress, May 10, 1776. Volume 4. Library of Congress, 1906, Hathi Trust Digital Library, page 342. Accessed October 2018 to July 2020. https://babel.hathitrust.org/cgi/pt?id=hvd.32044020407417&view=1up&seq=348.

Journals of the Continental Congress, January 30, 1783, Volume 24. Library of Congress 1922, HathiTrust Digital Library, page 102. Accessed April 2019. https://babel.hathitrust.org/cgi/pt?id=msu.31293020542753&view=1up&seq=116.

Journals of the Continental Congress, March 28, 1785, Volume 28. Library of Congress 1933, HathiTrust Digital Library, page 202. Accessed August 2019. https://babel.hathitrust.org/cgi/pt?id=hvd.32044116229097&view=1up&seq=218&q1=apprehend%20AND%20it%20AND%20will.

Journals of the Continental Congress, February 21, 1787, Volume 32. Library of Congress 1936, HathiTrust Digital Library, page 74. Accessed July 2019. https://babel.hathitrust.org/cgi/pt?id=msu.31293104451897&view=1up&seq=92.

Journals of the Continental Congress, September 28, 1787. Volume 33. Library of Congress 1936, HathiTrust Digital Library, page 549. Accessed May 2019. https://babel.hathitrust.org/cgi/pt?id=msu.31293020682328&view=1up&seq=177.

King, Jr., Martin Luther. 1963. "'I Have A Dream' speech." Accessed March 2019 to July 2020. https://ourlutherking.com/i-have-a-dream-speech-text/.

"Legislation of the United Kingdom: subordinate legislation." British Library. Accessed October 2018. https://www.bl.uk/voices-of-science/britishlibrary/~/media/subjects%20images/government%20publications/pdfs/subordinate-leg.

"Letter from Benjamin Franklin to Lord Kames, 3 January 1760." National Archives. Accessed March 2019. https://founders.archives.gov/documents/Franklin/01-09-02-0002 viewed March 2019.

"Letter from General Churchill to James II, 23 November 1688." The Jacobite Heritage. Accessed July to September 2018. http://www.jacobite.ca/documents/1688churchill.htm.

"Letter from Lord Dartmouth to Governor Gage lamenting the behaviour of the House of Representatives and the mob, August 3, 1774." University of Chicago Library, from the National Archives. Accessed January 2019. http://pi.lib.uchicago.edu/1001/cat/bib/11585240.

"Letter from the Earl of Dartmouth, Secretary of State for the Colonies, to the Hon. Governor Gage, Whitehall, April 9, 1774." in *The Parliamentary History of England, from the earliest period to the year 1803*, volume 18 (London: T. C. Hansard, 1813), 75–7. Accessed Hathi Trust Digital Library January 2019. https://babel.hathitrust.org/cgi/pt?id=umn.31951d01078685f&view=1up&seq=59.

"Letter of invitation to William of Orange, 1688." The Jacobite Heritage. Accessed August 2018. http://jacobite.ca/documents/16880630.htm.

Lindert, Peter H., and Jeffrey G. Williamson. "American Incomes 1774–1860," NBER Working Paper No. 18396, issued in September 2012. National Bureau of Economic Research's Development of the American Economy programme. Accessed November 29, 2018. https://www.nber.org/papers/w18396.

Locke, John. 1689. "A Letter Concerning Toleration." Accessed August 2018. Internet Archive: https://archive.org/details/toleration/mode/2up.

Lovejoy, David S. 1972. *The Glorious Revolution in America*. Harper & Row.

Madison, James. "Notes on the Debates in the Federal Convention 1787, May 29." The Avalon Project, Yale Law School. Accessed July 2019. https://avalon.law.yale.edu/18th_century/debates_529.asp.

Madison, James. "Notes on the Debates in the Federal Convention 1787, June 6." The Avalon Project, Yale Law School. Accessed April 2019. https://avalon.law.yale .edu/18th_century/debates_606.asp.

Madison, James. "Notes on the Debates in the Federal Convention 1787, July 6." The Avalon Project, Yale Law School. Accessed April 2019. https://avalon.law.yale .edu/18th_century/debates_705.asp.

Madison, James. "Notes on the Debates in the Federal Convention 1787, July 16." The Avalon Project, Yale Law School. Accessed July 2019. https://avalon.law .yale.edu/18th_century/debates_716.asp.

Madison, James. "Notes on the Debates in the Federal Convention 1787, August 21." The Avalon Project, Yale Law School. Accessed August 2019. https://avalon.law .yale.edu/18th_century/debates_821.asp.

Madison, James. "Notes on the Debates in the Federal Convention 1787, August 22." The Avalon Project, Yale Law School. Accessed June 2019. https://avalon.law .yale.edu/18th_century/debates_822.asp.

Madison, James. "Notes on the Debates in the Federal Convention 1787, September 7." The Avalon Project, Yale Law School. Accessed June 2019. https://avalon.law .yale.edu/18th_century/debates_907.asp.

Madison, James. "Notes on the Debates in the Federal Convention 1787, September 17." The Avalon Project, Yale Law School. Accessed June 2019. https://avalon .law.yale.edu/18th_century/debates_917.asp.

Madison, James. "Proposed Amendment of Articles of Confederation," [12 March] 1781. National Archives. Accessed August 2019. https://founders.archives.gov /documents/Madison/01-03-02-0007.

"Magna Carta, 1215." London: British Museum, 1963, translated by Davis, G. R. C., pp. 23–33, published online by the British Library. Accessed July 2018. https:// www.bl.uk/magna-carta/articles/magna-carta-english-translation#.

"Magna Carta, 1297." 25_Edw_1_cc_1_9_29. legislation.gov.uk. Accessed July to September 2018. https://www.legislation.gov.uk/aep/Edw1cc1929/25/9/introduc tion.

Maitland, F. W. 1908. Lectures given in 1888. *The Constitutional History of England.* Cambridge University Press.

"Manuscript copy of the minutes of the first meeting of the Boston on Committee of Correspondence, Nov. 3, 1772." Collection of the New York Public Library. Accessed February 2019. https://www.nypl.org/blog/2015/11/30/boston-commit tee-documents.

McHenry, James. "Papers of Dr. James McHenry on the Federal Convention of 1787." The Avalon Project, Yale Law School. Accessed August 2019. https:// avalon.law.yale.edu/18th_century/mchenry.asp.

Milsom, S. F. C. 2003. *A Natural History of the Common Law.* Columbia University Press.

Mitchell, B. R. 1988. *British Historical Statistics.* Cambridge University Press.

Natleson, Robert G. 2013. "Founding-Era Conventions and the meaning of The Constitution's 'Convention for proposing Amendments.'" *Florida Law Review* 65 (May 2013 Number 3): 644.

"On Elections to Parliament: 8 Henry VI (1429)." Constitution Society. Accessed September 2018. http://constitution.org/sech/sech_069.htm.

"Ordinance and Constitution of the Treasurer, Council, and Company in England, for a Council of State and General Assembly. 1621." The Avalon Project, Yale Law School. Accessed March to July 2020. https://avalon.law.yale.edu/17th_century/va04.asp.

Paine, Thomas. 1776. *Common Sense: addressed to the Inhabitants of America.* R, Bell, Philadelphia.

Perkins, Edward J. 1994. *American Public Finance and Financial Services 1700–1815.* Ohio State University Press.

"Petition of Right, 1628." The National Archives (U.K.). Accessed June to September 2018. http://www.nationalarchives.gov.uk/pathways/citizenship/rise_parliament/transcripts/petition_right.htm.

Pincus, Steven. 2009. *1688: The First Modern Revolution.* Yale University Press.

"Population in the Colonial and Continental Periods." The United States Census Bureau. Accessed February 2019 to July 2020. https://www.census.gov/history/pdf/colonialbostonpops.pdf.

"Prince of Orange's declaration: 19 December 1688." *Journal of the House of Commons*: Volume 10, 1688–1693 (London, 1802), pp. 1–6. British History Online. Accessed June to August 2018. http://www.british-history.ac.uk/commons-jrnl/vol10/pp1-6.

"Proceedings of a Convention of Delegates . . . Held at Boston August 3–9, 1780." J. Munsell, 1867, 50. Accessed July 2019. https://babel.hathitrust.org/cgi/pt?id=loc.ark:/13960/t5db8pn1n&view=1up&seq=58.

"Proceedings of Commissioners to remedy Defects of the Federal Government, Annapolis, September 11, 1786." The Avalon Project, Yale Law School. Accessed August 2019. https://avalon.law.yale.edu/18th_century/annapoli.asp.

"Proclamation, For Suppressing Rebellion and Sedition August 23, 1776." National Archives. Accessed November 2018 to July 2020. https://www.archives.gov/historical-docs/todays-doc/?dod-date=823.

Rabushka, Alvin. 2008. *Taxation in Colonial America.* Princeton University Press.

"Ratification of the Constitution by the State of Massachusetts, February 6, 1788." The Avalon Project, Yale Law School. Accessed May 2019. https://avalon.law.yale.edu/18th_century/ratma.asp.

"Ratification of the Constitution by the State of New Hampshire, June 21, 1788." The Avalon Project, Yale Law School. Accessed August 2019. https://avalon.law.yale.edu/18th_century/ratnh.asp.

"Ratification of the Constitution by the State of Virginia, June 26, 1788." The Avalon Project, Yale Law School. Accessed April 2019. https://avalon.law.yale.edu/18th_century/ratva.asp.

"Reports of the Committee of Secrecy to the Honourable House of Commons, relating to the late South-Sea directors, &c. 1721." Cato, London. Accessed September 2018. https://archive.org/details/pp1312061-2001/page/n0.

"Resolutions of the Continental Congress October 19, 1765." The Avalon Project, Yale Law School. Accessed March 2019. https://avalon.law.yale.edu/18th_century/resolu65.asp.

"Resolutions of the Virginia Convention, August 1–6, 1774." The Avalon Project, Yale Law School. Accessed March 2019. https://avalon.law.yale.edu/18th_century/assoc_of_va_conv_1774.asp.

Robertson, Geoffrey. 2005. *The Tyrannicide Brief. The Story of the Man Who Sent Charles I to the Scaffold.* Chatto & Windus.

"Second Charter of Virginia, 1609." The Avalon Project, Yale Law School. Accessed March 2019 to July 2020. https://avalon.law.yale.edu/17th_century/va02.asp.

Siedentop, Larry. 2014. *Inventing the Individual: the origins of Western Liberalism.* Allen Lane.

"Speech Of the Right Honorable The Earl of Chatham, In the House of Lords, Jan. 20, 1775." Evans American Early Imprint Collection, University of Michigan Library. Accessed September 2018 to July 2020. https://quod.lib.umich.edu/e/evans/N11390.0001.001?rgn=main;view=fulltext.

Stuart, James (King James VI of Scotland and James I of England). *The Trve Lawe of free Monarchies: Or, The Reciprock and Mvtvall Dvtie Betwixt a free King, and his naturall Subjectes.* London, 1616: British Library. Accessed July 2018. https://www.bl.uk/collection-items/the-true-law-of-free-monarchies-by-king-james-vi-and-i.

Translations and Reprints from the Original Sources of European history, 1897. Translated by E. P. Cheyney, University of Pennsylvania Press. Accessed August 2018. Fordham University: https://sourcebooks.fordham.edu/source/ed1-summons.asp.

"Treaty of Paris 1763." The Avalon Project, Yale Law School. Accessed November 2018 to July 2020. https://avalon.law.yale.edu/subject_menus/constpap.asp.

Washington, George. 1789. "First inaugural address as President." The Avalon Project, Yale Law School. Accessed July 2019. https://avalon.law.yale.edu/18th_century/wash1.asp.

Washington, George. "Letter of the President of the Federal Convention, Dated September 17, 1787, to the President of Congress, Transmitting the Constitution." The Avalon Project, Yale Law School. Accessed August 2019. https://avalon.law.yale.edu/18th_century/translet.asp.

"William and Mary, 1688: An Act declareing the Rights and Liberties of the Subject and Setleing the Succession of the Crowne." [Chapter II. Rot. Parl. pt. 3. nu. 1.] in *Statutes of the Realm*: Volume 6, 1685–94, ed. John Raithby (s.l, 1819), British History Online, 142–145. Accessed August 17, 2018. http://www.british-history.ac.uk/statutes-realm/vol6/pp142-145.

"William and Mary, 1688: An Act for Establishing the Coronation Oath." [Chapter VI. Rot. Parl. pt. 5. nu. 3.] in *Statutes of the Realm*: Volume 6, 1685–94, ed. John Raithby (s.l, 1819), pp. 56–57. British History Online. Accessed July to October 2018. https://www.british-history.ac.uk/statutes-realm/vol6/pp56-57.

Wood, Gordon S. 1969. *The Creation of the American Republic.* The University of North Carolina Press.

Further Reading

Adams, Willi Paul. 1980. *The First American Constitutions*. The University of North Carolina Press.

Attenborough, F.L. 1922. *The Laws of the Earliest English Kings*. Cambridge University Press.

Berkin, Carol. 2003: first published 2002. *A brilliant Solution: inventing the American Constitution*. Mariner Books.

Black, Jeremy. Blog post April 24, 2013. "George III and his Prime Ministers." Accessed October 2018. https://history.blog.gov.uk/2013/04/24/george-iii-and-his-prime-ministers/.

Broadberry, Stephen; Campbell, Bruce M. S.; and van Leeuwen, Bas. 2010. "English Medieval Population: Reconciling Time Series and Cross-Sectional Evidence." University of Warwick, Department of Economics. https://warwick.ac.uk/fac/soc/economics/staff/sbroadberry/wp/medievalpopulation7.pdf.

de Tocqueville, Alexis (author), and Harvey C. Mansfield and Delba Winthrop (trans. and eds.). First published 1835, this edition 2000. *Democracy in America*. University of Chicago Press.

Edling, Max M. 2018. *The Creation of the Constitution: New Essays on American Constitutional History*. American Historical Association.

Gallay, Alan. 2019. *Walter Raleigh: Architect of Empire*. Basic Books.

Ginsburg, The Hon. Douglas H. 2015. "Discovery and Creation in the Law." Centre for Independent Studies. Accessed Attended in 2015, viewed in October 2018. https://www.youtube.com/watch?v=k4rJSD5DLno.

Gneist, Rudolph; translated by Ashworth, Phillip A. Second edition, 1889. *The History of the English Constitution*. William Clowes and Sons Limited.

Gray, Edward G. and Kamensky, James (editors). 2013. *The Oxford Handbook of the American Revolution*. Oxford University Press.

Halstead, T.J. June 23, 1999. "The Separation of Powers Doctrine: An Overview of its Rationale And Application." CRS Report for Congress. http://congressionalresearch.com/RL30249/document.php#:~:text=The%20Separation%20of%20

Powers%20Doctrine%3A%20An%20Overview%20of,exercise%20of%20 power%20by%20any%20single%20ruling%20body.

Hamilton, Alexander; Madison, James; and Jay, John. Edited by Hamilton, John C. First published 1787–88; this edition 1909. *The Federalist. A Commentary on the Constitution of the United States*. J.B. Lippincott Company.

Jensen, Merrill. 1958. *The New Nation: A History of the United States During the Confederation 1781–1789*. Alfred A. Knopf.

Kammen, Michael (editor). 1986. *The origins of the American Constitution—a documentary history*. Penguin Books.

Klarman, Michael J. 2016. *The Framers' Coup: The Making of the United States Constitution*. Oxford University Press.

Klerman, Daniel. January 2000. "Settlement and the Decline of Private Prosecution in Thirteenth-Century England." (Independent Institute Working Paper #19). Accessed October 2018. http://www.independent.org/pdf/working_papers/19_settlement.pdf.

Levy, Leonard W. 1999. *Origins of the Bill of Rights*. Yale University Press.

Maddison, Angus. 2001. *The World Economy: a Millennial Perspective*. OECD Development Centre.

McAuley, Finbarr. Autumn, 2006. "Canon Law and the End of the Ordeal." *Oxford Journal of Legal Studies*, Vol. 26, No. 3 pp. 473–513.

Middlekauf, Robert. 1982. *The Glorious Cause – The American Revolution 1763–1789*. Oxford University Press.

Natelson, Robert G. Volume 65 May 2013 Number 3. "Founding-Era Conventions and the Meaning of The Constitution's 'Convention for Proposing Amendments.'" *Florida Law Review*. Accessed June 2019. http://www.floridalawreview.com/2013/robert-g-natelsonfounding-era-conventions-and-the-meaning-of-the-constitutions-convention-for-proposing-amendments/.

Pestana, C.G. 2004. *The English Atlantic in the Age of Revolution 1640–1661*. Harvard University Press.

Plucknett, T.F.T. 1956. *A Concise History of the Common Law*. 5th edition, Butterworth & Co. (Publishers) Ltd.

Scott, Jonathan. 2019. *How the Old World Ended—The Anglo-Dutch-American Revolution, 1500–1800*. Yale University Press.

Sharma, Simon. 2009. *A History of Britain: the British Wars*. The Bodley Head.

Womersley, David. 2015. *James II: The Last Catholic King*. Penguin.

Wood, Gordon S. December 30, 2010. "'The Great American Argument' Gordon S. Wood's review of "Ratification: The People Debate the Constitution, 1787–1788" by Pauline Maier." *The New Republic*. Accessed March 2019. https://newrepublic.com/article/79740/great-american-argument-ratification.

Index

About the Author

James Philips studied at the Universities of Oxford and Sydney, and he holds degrees in liberal arts and in law. He has been a successful mergers and acquisitions attorney for more than thirty years and is a visiting lecturer at the University of Sydney's Law School. He held leadership positions at two law firms and is now a non-executive director of several organizations, including a leading Australian public-policy-research institute. He first read the American Constitution in school, and began reading about the English revolutionary and American colonial periods in 2005.